DE PROPRIETATIBUS LITTERARUM

edenda curat

C. H. VAN SCHOONEVELD

Indiana University

Series Maior, 2

THE
EPIC VOICE

by

RODNEY DELASANTA

Providence College

1967

MOUTON

THE HAGUE · PARIS

Printed in The Netherlands by Mouton & Co., Printers, The Hague.

To Homer and Paul
who started it all

ACKNOWLEDGEMENTS

Perhaps there are certain debts which creditors would prefer to leave unpaid. I suspect that in a book's case the academic creditors would rather wait for the reviews before they are identified, but the exigencies of publication force the debtor to pay his debts publicly and in advance. To Professors Edward A. Bloom and Andrew J. Sabol of Brown University, who supervised this study as a dissertation and prodded it out of "uncouth form" into "comely rew", and to Professor John Workman for his kind encouragement, I owe special gratitude. To my colleagues, Professors Mario L. D'Avanzo and Rene E. Fortin, who suffered my gestative pains when they would have preferred suffering their own; to my typist, Mrs. Jo-Ann Elias DiNunzio, who cheerfully submitted to my petulant tyrannies; and finally to my wife and children whose unmistakable presence interrupted my efforts repeatedly enough to remind me of my first loves – I am also grateful.

R. K. D.

Providence College
Providence, R.I.
May, 1967

TABLE OF CONTENTS

I. INTRODUCTION

1

The purpose of this study is to bring the discipline of modern narrative criticism to an ancient and respected – but often neglected – genre: the epic poem. Much of the criticism that has touched on the epic since the "epomaniac" days of the eighteenth century, when it has not been cultural, has been eulogistic and honorific. Like a favorite but aged mistress, the epic has been accorded by some critics merely sentimental and nostalgic attention. For others, the periphery of epic has proved more fruitful of study than the great work itself. Archaeology, anthropology, linguistics, history – although they have proved to be of extraordinary value to the ancillary study of the epic poem – cannot be confused or equated with literary study *per se*. Even the field of comparative oral literature that has made spectacular advances with its theory of oral formulaic composition in the heroic poem has not yet published the results of its discoveries in any prolific way. Fortunately, some scholars have recently begun to recognize the epic acreage that lies untilled and have decided to put their hands to the plow.[1] My own book, hopefully, will add another modest furrow to that field which has lain fallow too long.

In general, this study will look at some of the "classical" epic works of our language by focusing on that substantial intention of the genre that makes all its accidental intentions meaningful – the artistry of narration. The only real reason for the survival of the great epic poems, after all, can be traced not primarily to their authors' physics or metaphysics, ethics or politics, rhetoric or poetic – but rather to their skill as narrative artists. That skill, although different in degree from those

---

[1] The scholarly names that will recur throughout this study make a preliminary and perfunctory introduction here unnecessary. Tillyard, Lewis, Whitman, Mac-Affrey, Ferry, Greene and company will take their bibliographic bows later.

qualities of narrative artistry that characterize our modern short stories and novels, must in some manner share those strategies of narration which have been the common property of story tellers from earliest times. Although, for example, modern literature reveals an obvious predilection for "showing", as opposed to the classical preference for "telling", still the language which critics have invented to describe the show-tell distinction has tended too often to suggest that modern fiction is contemptuous of the latter and that classical fiction was incapable of the former. As Wayne Booth's recent book has served to correct our comfortable disdain of "telling" and to reinstate its value as a device even of modern fiction,[2] so it is my intention – hopefully – to demonstrate that "showing", particularly as it relates to the problems of restricted point of view, did not come into being when the language of criticism describing it was invented but actually is as old as Homer. The Oedipus complex existed before Freud, Sophocles and even Oedipus himself. Similarly, the problem of who is telling the story to whom and by what mouthpiece antedated the critics who decided to call this confrontation between writer, speaker, and internal and external audience *point of view*, or *register of consciousness,* or *focus of narration*, or *voice.*

Because it is the particular intention of this study to trace an *in medias res* tradition from its inception in Homer to its English flowering in Milton by means of a critical strategy made popular by the terms above, it is desirable that I make more precise our metaphors for that strategy by tailoring them to the peculiar needs of epic narration. *Voice* will recur frequently here because the implications of its metaphor are suitable to the assumptions of this study. If E.M.W. Tillyard is correct in designating *control* (pre-determination or sustained effort of the will as opposed to exuberance, however ingenious) as one of the indispensable characteristics of epic,[3] then the metaphor of *voice* will more meaningfully reflect that control than, for example, the metaphor of *point of view*. The latter, although it has been the more commonly used term and although I shall have some occasion to use it, carries with it enough weaknesses to be of limited value; for nowhere in the analogy of the vantage point of the seeing speaker (his view extended or restricted by the point he commits himself to) does the idea of *control* predominate. Even when his point of view is omniscient, when he makes apparent most openly his ability to see god-like into the total involvement of the

²   *The Rhetoric of Fiction* (Chicago, 1961).
³   *The English Epic and Its Background* (London, 1954), pp. 8-12.

action, there is nothing in the metaphor to suggest the transcendental, sustaining relationship between author and his creation that the epic demands. Point of view here suggests a kind of narrative foreknowledge without the accompanying providence.

It would seem, then, that the weakness of this metaphor (and its cognates like *focus* of narration) lies in the sight analogy to which it is committed. Perhaps it can be strengthened and complemented by the metaphor of sound, of voice, which though certainly not original here, may obviate a multitude of metaphorical problems. Certainly the quality of passivity common to all the sight metaphors would not weaken the voice analogy. The articulated voice is an active agent, an objectification of thought emanating from it and calling to attention those objects which in the course of the artist's creation are subject to its power. The artist's voice is heard authoritatively as a subject hears its master and obeys it. Or, more precisely, since the artist is the supreme being of his own creation, his voice not only commands obedience but serves as the active agent – the *fiat* – of creation. Hence, no matter what the inflections of voice may suggest, the *voice* is in actuality always all-powerful, always in control, even though it may, when it desires to tease us out of thought, choose to affect limitation and restriction.[4] Like the God of Revelation, the artist may decide to reveal himself in the voice of omniscient authority. Or like the same God hidden in nature who affects circumscription by his own creation, the artist may decide to restrict his authority and subject it to the limitations of his creatures.

How many voices can be identified in a work of fiction? Recent scholars, in recognizing the control that voice wields over most ingredients of narrative, have worked hard in distinguishing among many varieties.[5] But despite their useful cataloguing, voice in the final analysis can be distinguished only into two real kinds: the voice that speaks with total knowledge (or presumes to) and the voice that does not (or presumes not to); the voice of omniscience and the voice of restriction. The problem, of course, is complex because it involves the critic with disci-

---

[4]   Or as Wayne Booth has phrased it: ". . . though the author can to some extent choose his disguises, he can never choose to disappear." (p. 20).
[5]   The classical studies in this area are Henry James, *The Art of the Novel: Critical Prefaces*, ed. R. P. Blackmur (New York, 1934) and Percy Lubbock, *The Craft of Fiction* (New York, 1921). The most useful bibliography has been compiled by Norman Friedman, "Point of View in Fiction: The Development of a Critical Concept", *PMLA*, LXX (Dec., 1955), 1160-1184. The most provocative and valuable recent book, of course, is Wayne Booth, *The Rhetoric of Fiction* (Chicago, 1961), pp. 149-165.

plines like psychology, epistemology, and even theology. The omniscient voice, after all, in order to be omniscient must either be divine, or inspired by divinity, or deluded into pretensions of divinity. The restricted voice, on the other hand, must recognize its epistemological limitations and the inviolability and inaccessibility of another's consciousness. Thus, the extension of omniscience in one direction and restriction in the opposite direction would involve voice at one extreme – its most divine – in revelation and oracle and at the other extreme – its most human – in self-delusion and even prevarication.

Epic from time immemorial has been regarded as the great vehicle for omniscient voice. If we can believe Northrop Frye that epic is a post-mythic genre which preserves a significant residue of divine story,[6] then the voice that can articulate truths about divinity or even heroic humanity descended from divinity must somehow operate with divine sanction. Hence, the inspiration of the Muses of which Plato speaks in the *Ion* cannot have been considered entirely hyperbolic: ". . . God takes away the minds of poets, and uses them as his ministers, as he also uses diviners and holy prophets, in order that we who hear them may know them to be speaking not of themselves who utter these priceless words in a state of unconsciousness, but that God himself is the speaker, and that through them he is conversing with us." [7] Nor should we be cynical about Renaissance epic poets who obviously inherited the formula of inspiration more as convention than as supplication. Milton's invocation to the Holy Spirit, for example, is fully consonant with Christian beliefs about divine inspiration. Certainly, Anne Davidson Ferry's recent study of the narrator in *Paradise Lost* makes it clear that the narrator (if not the poet) "claims the instruction granted to Moses and the illumination granted the blind man".[8]

Yet the epic poem is *not* myth, however descended its genealogy may be from that genre. Recent scholars have written well about the narrowing or limiting of the shamanistic or mythical hero into the epic protagonist. C. M. Bowra, Gertrude R. Levy, and Northrop Frye have recently been grouped and aided by Thomas Greene who recognizes that the epic hero in having been transformed from the state of shaman or god has experienced a "diminishing of his capacities to approximate more

[6]   *The Anatomy of Criticism* (Princeton, 1957), p. 35.
[7]   *The Dialogues of Plato*, trans. Benjamin Jowett (*Great Books of the Western World*, No. 7) (Chicago, 1952), p. 144.
[8]   *Milton's Epic Voice* (Cambridge, Mass., 1963), p. 24.

closely those wc know".[9] Greene sees these critics as agreeing that the epic is not "an attempt to inflate the hero's naturally meager capacities" but rather the opposite: to celebrate a heroism severely limited by his humanity.[10] Frye's distinction between the romance hero (who is superior not only to his fellow men but to his environment as well) and the epic hero (who is superior to his fellow men but *not* to his environment or their social criticism and thus subject to the "mortalizing" limitations of nature and men) is also appropriate here.[11] Thus, although the epic hero leaves us with a human *awe*, the object of that awe remains essentially *human*. In Greene's words, "epic awe, as distinguished from religious or mythic awe, springs from the realization that a man can commit an extraordinary act while still remaining limited".[12]

Translated into the exigencies of epic narrative art, the human awe requires a duality of vehicles. On the one hand, the residue of divinity remaining in any epic poem requires a voice expansive enough to climb above the Aonian Mount and authoritative enough to be totally believed even when it penetrates to the remote corners of heaven. Thus, although the omniscient speaker of *Paradise Lost* is a fallen man, his inspiration by divinity assures him of an authority, certitude and omniscience greater even than the angelic voice of Raphael who, as we shall see, does *not* know all things. On the other hand, the human limitations inherent in the epic form demand a lesser voice, one which will complement the omniscient but in a manner subject to and circumscribed by those limitations. The *nuntius*, therefore, who is a staple of *in medias res* epic, is more than an accident of epic narration. His voice operates as the necessary limitation upon the quasi-divinity of omniscient narration, constantly reminding the reader by its very presence of the essential humanity of epic heroism. Ulysses, Aeneas, Musidorus and Pyrocles, the host of nuntii from the *Faerie Queene*, Adam, and even the Archangel Raphael himself (who though more than human is less than divine) – all restricted voices impinging upon the omniscience of their respective epics – introduce the strategy of restricted narration into Western Literature. The artistic effect of this strategy on the individual epics to be considered will constitute the major business of this study. Whether later fiction was touched by this epic convention is a problem to be

[9] For a discussion of their respective contributions to the problem, see Thomas Greene, *The Descent from Heaven, A Study in Epic Continuity* (New Haven, 1963), p. 12 ff.
[10] Greene, p. 13.
[11] Frye, p. 34.
[12] Greene, p. 15.

deferred for further study. But it is fascinating to consider that the splendid first-person narration of Ulysses in the *Odyssey* might conceivably be related by the genealogy of epic continuity to other narrations and other odysseys. Huck Finn and Captain Marlow are heroes of another vintage, but as narrator-mariners of their own novels the new wine seems to have been poured in old bottles.

2

To what extent does the epic poet's commitment to a dual voice determine the structural dimensions of his work? How much is the textural artistry of epic narration affected by the intrusion of restricted voice upon the omniscient? The answers to these questions will actually inform the organization of this study, particularly as they relate to that specific kind of epic that older critics have designated as *in medias res*. But before this central thesis can be developed, it will be necessary to distinguish among the kinds of epic to be considered here in order to identify the relationship of intention to voice, to recognize that the traditions and conventions of the genre a poet inherits largely determine his artistic commitment to this or that kind of narrative. Although, for example, *Beowulf*, *The Faerie Queene* and *Paradise Lost* have all been called epics, it should be obvious even from a cursory reading that the species of epic each represents will wield a considerable influence upon the voice of the poem. Therefore, the following pages will be concerned with the nature of epic by attempting to distinguish among those substantial and accidental characteristics of the poem that have led critics to classify it into the traditional groupings of 1) the heroic poem, 2) the heroic romance or romantic epic, and 3) the literary epic.[13]

On the most basic level, the epic becomes distinguished from other kinds of literature first by its material cause (the author's reaction to experience) and then by its final and formal causes. Whereas the lyric records the inward cry of the poet at his most individual state, at his most proximate reaction to experience, the epic records, more expansively and with a more highly developed fiction, the judgment of the poet at his most social state, at his most detached and most complex reaction to experience. It is this social intention, moreover, the epic poet's conscious integration of an audience into his experience, that differentiates epic

---

[13] I risk here a certain tedium that necessarily results from reviewing established or quasi-established ideas. Although the distinctions are important in developing my thesis later, those readers who already feel comfortable with the distinctions may wish to move ahead to Section 3 of this chapter.

from lyric on the level of final, as well as material, cause. Unlike the lyric poet who, jealous of his individuality, allows his audience only to overhear, the epic poet requires that his audience prepare for his performance and consciously attempt to "assist" at his recital. In this respect, as C. S. Lewis points out,[14] the epic, unlike the lyric, demands a quasi-ritualistic occasion. Northrop Frye, too, finds a metaphor from religion useful. For him, lyric is to epic as prayer is to sermon.[15]

As we investigate the phrase "with a more highly developed fiction", we turn from the final cause of the epic to its formal cause. Although most critics insist on the essentially fictional nature of all literature, we can assert without offending even the Crocean theorist that the complexities of fiction in the epic set it off from the lyric. In Northrop Frye's terms, the epic contains not only an external fiction, which establishes a relationship between the author and his society, but also relies for its primary interest on its internal fiction, which implies a relationship between the hero and his society.[16] It is true that even in lyric the writer is to some extent a fictional hero with a fictional audience,[17] but the primary interest there is *dianoia*, and not *mythos*. The formal distinction then between epic and lyric is plot, *dianoia* in epic being subordinate to, or at least consequent upon, *mythos*.

But the epic genre, large as it may be, cannot be equated simply with all poetry of *mythos*. Unless we wish to throw up our hands and repeat with Benedetto Croce that literary genres do not exist at all, it will be necessary to distinguish among various species within the genus epic. To call both *Beowulf* and *Paradise Lost* epics, after all, is to stretch the limits of the term until it includes both the oral formulaic narrative of an heroic age and a highly sophisticated literary production of a very unheroic age. A further complication arises here too when one recalls that the great narrative poem of the Middle Ages, the romance, intervenes historically between the heroic poem of the heroic ages and the literary epic of the Renaissance. By the sixteenth century in Italy and England, the romance has become crossed with the classical type of literary epic and assumes a distinctively hybrid character which is reflected in its name – the heroic romance or the romantic epic. Thus, the generic term

---

[14] C. S. Lewis, *A Preface to Paradise Lost* (Oxford, 1942), p. 17.
[15] Frye, p. 249.
[16] Frye, pp. 52-53.
[17] Frye explains that "a poet sending a love poem to his lady complaining of her cruelty has stereoscoped his four ethical elements into two but the four are still there".

epic contains these three species whose relationships and distinctions concern us here.

Let us first attempt to define the kind of poem represented by *Beowulf* and the *Chanson de Roland* by distinguishing it from that represented by *Havelock the Dane* and *Sir Gawain and the Green Knight*. To eliminate confusion between terms that designate the "great" poem of the heroic ages and the "great" poem of the Renaissance and Neo-Classic Ages, the former shall be referred to as *heroic poem* and the latter as *literary epic,* the prototype of the heroic poem being the *Iliad* and of the epic the *Aeneid*. Historically, in the development of a national literature, the heroic poem always precedes the romance, and if the latter does not completely supplant the former (as it does in English poetry), the heroic poem co-exists for a while with the romance (as it does with the *Chanson de Roland* and other chansons de gestes) and finally bastardizes its heroic qualities altogether. Furthermore, the heroic poem is an indigenous creation produced, preserved, and perpetuated by a people celebrating in the figure of its hero some ethnic quality sacred to them. Although one remembers that the setting of Beowulf is not Angleland but Gautland and Denmark, still the ethnic memory, isolated from and uncorrupted by alien cultures, is capable of responding to the slightest allusion and the most distant digression in spite of the poem's transplantation across the sea. The romance, on the other hand, begins to be created in point of time when foreign cultures engulf the isolated culture, bringing with them tides of alien literary subject matter. Except for the Matter of England, the subject of medieval English romance is foreign: the Matter of Britain (with its Arthurian legends more Celtic and French than Anglo-Saxon), the Matter of France, and the Matter of Rome. Thus, the heroic narrative of one culture, when transplanted across distances, may become the romance of another.[18]

Thematically too the heroic poem is distinguishable from the romance. Although both types are metrical narratives dealing with works of heroic adventure and achievement, the heroic poet prefers a martial subject untouched by the amatory, whereas the romance mixes the adventurous with the amatory, the latter often motivating the former. Thus the heroic poem is essentially virile and serious, demanding active attention from its auditors; the romance is feminine and diverting, expecting little more than audition.

The most important distinction, however, is that of contemporary

[18] Nathaniel Griffin, "Definition of Romance", *PMLA*, XXXVIII (March, 1923), 56 ff.

probability. Romance thrives on tales of improbability or incredibility *which its auditors recognize to be improbable or incredible*. Certainly the fourteenth-century audience of *Sir Gawain and the Green Knight* did not believe that a decapitated knight could pick up his head and ride away. The events of an heroic poem, on the other hand, are credible, or at least did not demand a violent suspension of disbelief in its auditors. As Nathaniel Griffin points out:

The epic author [my distinction in terms Griffin obviously owes no allegiance to] and his contemporary auditors entertained a lively faith in the truth of the epic narrative, however improbably it may have been when regarded solely from the rationalistic standpoint. The epic poet never thinks of questioning in a spirit of semireligious seriousness in the full confidence that he will win a ready acquiescence from his hearers.[19]

W. P. Ker has offered us a convenient example of this distinction by discussing the heroic and romantic elements in *Beowulf* itself. Insisting that even for the auditors of its own day certain areas of Beowulf lent themselves to the fantastic whereas others were more worthy of verisimilitude, Ker uses the example of the Grendel combats:

The story of Beowulf and Grendel is not wildly fantastic or improbable; it agrees with the conditions of real life, as they have been commonly understood at all times except those of peculiar enlightenment and rationalism. It is not to be compared with the Phaeacian story of the adventures of Odysseus. Probably few of the earliest hearers of the Odyssey thought of the Sirens or of Calypso as anywhere near them while many of them must have had their grandmothers' testimony for things like the portents before the death of the suitors. Grendel in the poem of Beowulf is in the order of existence as these portents. If they are superstitions, they are among the most persistent; and they are superstitions rather than creatures of romance. ... [But] the episode of Grendel's mother is further from the matter of fact than the story of Grendel himself. ... Beowulf's descent under the water, his fight with the warlock's mother, the darkness of the "seadingle", the light of the mysterious sword; all this ... is far from Heorot and the report of the table-talk of Hrothgar, Beowulf and Unferth. It is also a different sort of thing from the fight with Grendel. There is more a supernatural incident, more romantic ornament, less of that concentration in the struggle which makes the fight with Grendel [a heroic rather than romantic encounter].[20]

As the fundamental distinctions between heroic poem and romance do not obscure the historical relationships of one upon the other, neither do the more obvious distinctions between the romance and the epic cancel

19   Griffin, p. 56.
20   W. P. Ker, *Epic and Romance* (New York, 1957), pp. 171-172.

their historical relationships. It is true that the literary epic felt the main
stream of the heroic tradition directly, that Virgil, in using Homer, was
making literary and sophisticated for his own civilization what was oral
and bardic for the earlier culture. Yet, before the Homeric tradition
reached Virgil, it was modified and colored by the Greek romances, in
Virgil's case specifically by the *Argonautica* of Appolonius.[21] Interestingly enough, a close parallel reveals itself in non-classical Western literature, for Boiardo and Ariosto nourish themselves on the Roland poems
(all of which have their source in the heroic *Song of Roland*) as
Appolonius was nourished by Homer. And as the *Argonautica* grew
from the heroic poem and influenced greatly the Virgilian epic, so the
Ariostan romance grew from its heroic source in the *chansons de gestes*
to influence significantly the epics of Camöens and Tasso.[22] In English
literature, Spenser plays the role of intermediary by borrowing from the
romantic traditions of both his own literature and Ariosto and serving
deacon-like the high priest of the English epic – Milton.

But the species of epic represented by Spenser's poem is the central
problem here; and perhaps this is a task of definition more difficult than
the one just attempted, because the romantic epic is essentially a hybrid
work. Gabriel Harvey's reaction to the first draft of the *Faerie Queene*
– "Hobgoblin run away with the garland from Apollo" – at least rightly
understood Spenser's attempt to cross the narrative of Italian and
English romances with the high nationalistic seriousness of the Virgilian
epic. The result, of course, proves that the dominant genes of each type
somehow survived. From the romance in general came the characteristics
of story-for-its-own-sake, often improbably fraught with adventures and
amatory involvements. From the Italian epic in particular came the
Ariostan precedent of structural design by miscellaneity, the presence of
a number of heroes in the same long poem. From the literary epic came
the sense of high national purpose both "ancestrally" and teleologically
directed, as well as the sense of an *in medias res* structure that attempted
to lend unity to the Ariostan miscellaneity. In fact, the romantic epic's
peculiarity of structure, what C. S. Lewis calls "interlocked stories of
chivalrous adventure in a world of marvels",[23] is at the same time so un-
classical and classical that the real hybrid nature of the work manifests
itself extraordinarily here.

Certainly the profusion of characters suggests anything but a classical

---

[21] Tillyard, *The English Epic and its Background*, p. 61.
[22] C. M. Bowra, *From Virgil to Milton* (London, 1957), p. 18.
[23] C. S. Lewis, *The Allegory of Love* (New York, 1958), p. 308.

model. Their appearance and reappearance, threading their way into the fabric of various books, had no prototype in Virgil. And yet, at least in Books I and II where Red Cross and Guyon are the respective high mimetic heroes, we find a remarkable independent unity which, within the limits of each book, reminds one of the classical epic. It would be absurd to claim that Spenser wrote six different classical epics (especially when Books III, IV and V are so interdependent); but it would not be absurd to suggest that, judging from the architectonics of the first book, he would have known how to construct one had it been his intention. His total intention, however, depended upon a more encyclopedic than classically compact form, and so he produced smaller unities within a projected larger unity, a kind of super-epic. Certainly his projected use of the *in medias res* structure, as he describes it in his letter to Raleigh, and his real use of the *in medias res* within the limits of each work suggest some awareness of the classical model which Ariosto did not share.

Although *The Faerie Queene* has been chosen as the prime example of the romantic epic, one should not exclude here the prose type of romantic epic represented by Heliodorus's *Ethiopica* and Sidney's *Arcadia*. Like *The Faerie Queene*, they both blend the richness and variety of romance with nationalistic and didactic seriousness, but they differ enough from the *Faerie Queene* and from each other to make any all-inclusive definition of the romantic epic as type impossible. Suffice it to say that the species represents a mutation from the original epic gene, and that like most illegitimate offspring it defies exact classification.

If the catalogue of distinctions among heroic poem, romance, and romantic epic has been validly compiled up to here, the definition of literary epic remains before completion of the task. As in the previous pages, distinction will serve as the handmaiden of definition.

The most significant difference (and by now the most obvious) between the heroic poem and epic, as C. S. Lewis and C. M. Bowra point out, is that the former is oral and the latter written.[24] Whereas the heroic poet's intention in unlocking his word-hoard is essentially to aid the singer by way of oral formulas, the epic writer, concerned with the written line and not recitation, assumes a grandeur or "elevation" of style which takes the place of the ceremonial, ritualistic, recitative nature of the heroic poem.[25] In the epic "there are no external aids to

---

[24] Lewis, *A Preface to Paradise Lost*, Chapters III and VI and Bowra, *From Virgil to Milton*, Chapter I.
[25] Lewis, *Preface to Paradise Lost*, pp. 39-50.

solemnity which the Primary [heroic poem] enjoyed . . . no robed and garlanded *aoidos*, no altar, not even a feast in a hall – only a private person reading a book in an armchair. Yet somehow or other, that private person must be made to feel that he is assisting at an august ritual. . . . The sheer writing of the poem, therefore, must now do, of itself, what the whole occasion helped to do for Homer. The Virgilian and Miltonic style is there to compensate for – to counteract – the privacy and informality of silent reading in a man's study." [26]

Subject matter too reveals a basic difference between the heroic poem and epic. It is a gross over-simplification to point to the great national hero as the center of *all* "epics", to insist that the patriotic stirrings of a nation somehow become captured in these poems. Actually it is only the Virgilian and post-Virgilian epic and not the heroic poem that can answer totally to this demand. W. P. Ker, as long ago as 1896, recognized that the heroic poem was not primarily concerned with history but was in fact vague and general in relating itself to historic events:

The great historical names which appear in the old German heroic poetry are seldom found there in anything like their historical character, and not once in their chief historical aspect as adversaries of the Roman Empire.[27]

In the Greek heroic poem too the great subject is not one of its infallible identifying marks. Certainly the Trojan war cannot be considered the subject of the *Odyssey*; indeed it is not primarily the subject of the *Iliad*. If it were Homer's intention to celebrate the Greek victory in that mighty conflict, he would certainly not have broken off the story before the resolution, before the Trojan horse episode. As C. S. Lewis points out, the Trojan war is "merely the background of a purely personal story – that of Achilles' wrath, suffering, repentance, and killing of Hector".[28] And Robert Graves' new title for the *Iliad* – *The Anger of Achilles* – corroborates Lewis's point.

With the advent of the Virgilian epic, however, the celebration of the hero changes. No longer does the poet conceive of him as one who lives and dies for his own glory; the hero's glory is now tied to a cause outside of himself.

His life was no longer a short span . . . in the encompassing darkness, his duty no longer towards himself. From the eminence of his own glory he had

---

[26]   P. 39.
[27]   Ker, p. 22.
[28]   *Preface to Paradise Lost*, p. 27.

been reduced to a subordinate position where he was much inferior to the state or church to which he belonged.[29]

Seeking to celebrate the origins and present grandeur of Rome and at the same time to celebrate his patron Augustus, Virgil in the *Aeneid* lifted the Homeric poem from the level of primitive hero-worship to the level of the hero as representative of the race, to the hero as symbol not only of past but also of present and future glory. Henceforth, the heroes of epic poems conceived from Virgilian loins are not merely characters but exempla as well.

Naturally the explicitness or indirection of the exempla will largely determine the extent, if any, of allegory to be found in the epic. Le Bossu's definition of the epic — "un discours inventé avec art, pour former les moeurs par des instructions deguissés sous les allegoires d'une action importante" [30] — obviously bears more relevance to the kind of romantic epic we find in *The Faerie Queene* than what we find in the literary epic,[31] but the absence of continuous allegory in the latter does not preclude the possibility of what Frye calls "a freistimmige style in which allegory may be picked up and dropped again at pleasure".[32] At any rate, those poetic structures that dramatize political or religious doctrine are more characteristic of romantic and literary epics than they are of the heroic poem.

3

Although it is my intention to explore fully the functions of epic voice in those chapters dealing with individual epic poems, organizational propriety demands that I at least discuss it in general terms here: first, by marking characteristics of epic voice as it is determined by the different intentions of heroic poem, romantic epic and literary epic (already reviewed in section two); and then by listing general functions of the epic voice in anticipation of detailed treatment of individual works later.

It is a commonplace of literary criticism to characterize the point of view or voice proper to the epic poem as an arch-example of omniscient narration.[33] And yet any examination of the quality of omniscience

[29]   Bowra, p. 12.
[30]   *Traité du Poème Épique* (Paris, 1693), pp. 9-10, quoted by H. T. Swedenberg, *The Theory of the Epic in England, 1650-1800* (= *University of California Publications in English*, Vol. XV) (Berkeley, 1944), p. 155.
[31]   Bossu's definition, however, was of literary epic.
[32]   Frye, p. 90.
[33]   See Wayne Booth for a modern version of the traditional attitudes: pp. 4-6.

peculiar to each of the three species of epic will reveal that the breadth of omniscience implicitly claimed by the respective poets is significantly varied. The reasons for this variety seem directly related to the intention of each of the kinds. In the heroic poem, because the poet is moved to narrate primarily the exploits of a great hero and does not sing any substantial "extra-narrative" praise for prince or cause, voice assumes an omniscience limited by its own fictional circumference and, of course, conditioned by the mere physical demands of oral composition. The poet does indulge from time to time in short approbationary or disapprobationary statements of tone – "þat was god cyning" of *Beowulf* – but generally he is content to report the action and allow the narrative to stand by itself. Moreover, because his intention is primarily hero-centered and not ethno-centered, the heroic poet usually refrains from the kind of teleologizing that becomes such an important characteristic of the literary epic. The dipping into national prophecy found in Books VII and VIII of the *Aeneid*, Book X of the *Lusiad*, Books I and II of *The Faerie Queene*, and Books XI and XII of *Paradise Lost* is totally lacking in Homer or *Beowulf*. Nor does the tone of these works ever become nationalistically self-righteous, as the literary epic often does. The national hatred that Virgil assumes the Trojans (and by extension the Romans) must have felt for the Greeks (in *Aeneid* II) is simply never found operating, except of course in the heat of battle, in the heroic poem. Hector, after all, is the enemy in the *Iliad*, but Homer draws him more sympathetically than Achilles,[34] a gesture of generosity which Virgil did not repeat in his characterizations of Aeneas and Turnus. It is true that Turnus shows his virtues, but it is gross misreading to insist, as did Robert Southey, that Turnus is the more attractive character.[35] He is the enemy, noble but impedimental to the will of the gods, for whom the only just fate is death. Moreover, his death

---

[34] Cedric Whitman has worked out a convincing case for interpreting Achilles' wrath as heroically justifiable. See *Homer and the Heroic Tradition* (Cambridge, Mass., 1958), Chapter IX. This view runs in diametric opposition, of course, to that more standard attitude stated by C. M. Bowra in his *Tradition and Design in the Iliad* (Oxford, 1930), pp. 192-214, in which Achilles is taken to task for his behavior.

[35] "There are few readers who do not prefer Turnus to Aeneas – a fugitive, suspected of treason, who negligently left his wife, seduced Dido, deserted her, and then forcibly took Lavinia from her betrothed husband. What avails a man's piety to the Gods, if, in all his dealings with men, he proves himself a villain? If we represent Deity as commanding a bad action, this is not exculpating the man, but criminating the God." From the "Original Preface to *Joan of Arc*", in *The Poetical Works of Robert Southey* (New York, n.d.), p. 3.

resolves the great conflict between the Trojans and the Latins not merely in martial victory but *per omnia saecula saeculorum*. Because no such typological problem concerned Homer, he is more disposed to draw the combatants as they really existed in his imagination and not conditioned by what they should resemble in the ultimate political scheme of things. Achilles, the Greek, is bullheaded, jealous, wrathful and sulking, moved to heroic action not when the Greek ships are burning but only when his beloved Patroclus is slain. In fact, Achilles' saving grace is a less than heroic act – his responding to Priam's pathetic request to return Hector's desecrated body to Troy. Hector, the Trojan, is drawn with surprising respect, noble in almost every detail except for his all-too-human terror and flight at the moment before his death.

In both the romantic epic and literary epic, on the other hand, the quality of omniscience, because it is freed from the physical limitations of oral composition, extends beyond narrative and indulges in speculation sometimes only distantly related to the fiction. One has only to recall Virgil's nationalistic fervor, Sidney's and Spenser's intensive moralizing and Milton's personal lyricism to realize that, whatever the narrative intentions of these epic poems, the extra-narrative intentions, related as they are digressively to the narrative itself, demand a breadth of omniscience that far surpasses that of the heroic poem. Coleridge's famous letter to Cottle listing the necessary requirements of an epic poet reveals, despite its exaggerations, the degrees of omniscience an epic voice was expected to encompass. Writing of Southey's attempts at epic production, Coleridge says:

I am fearful that he will begin to rely too much on story and event in his poems, to the neglect of those lofty imaginings, that are peculiar to, and definitive of, the poet. The *story* of Milton might be told in two pages – it is this which distinguishes an Epic Poem from a Romance in metre. Observe the march of Milton – his severe application, his laborious polish, his deep metaphysical researches, his prayers to God before he began his great poem, all that could lift and swell his intellect, became his daily food. I should not think of devoting less than twenty years to an Epic Poem. Ten to collect materials and warm my mind with universal science. I would be a tolerable Mathematician, I would thoroughly know Mechanics, Hydrostatics, Optics and Astronomy, Botany, Metallurgy, Fossilism, Chemistry, Geology, Anatomy, Medicine – then the mind of man – then the minds of men – in all Travels, Voyages, and Histories. So I would spend ten years – the next five to the composition of the poem – and the last five to the correction of it.[36]

[36] *Unpublished Letters of Samuel Taylor Coleridge*, Vol. 1, ed. E. L. Griggs (New Haven, n.d.), pp. 71-72.

4

Having indicated generally the influence of "species" on voice, it now remains for me to generalize on the quality and function of the epic voice as it determines the structure of the epic poem.

So much has been written about the structure of the epic poem that most undergraduates know the cliches of epic criticism: unity of action, *in medias res*, fable, episode, digression. But nowhere has any critic explained the functional relationship of these terms to the structural center that supports them – the epic voice. Indeed, a brief review of the criticism that begot these terms will suggest that they perhaps will work more efficiently when they are in the company of, and reconciled to, the modern concepts of voice and point of view.

Unity of action, for example, mentioned first by Aristotle in the *Poetics* [37] and repeated religiously by almost every major Italian, French and English critic up to the nineteenth century, is a critical concept that insists on a poet keeping his plot limited to an appropriate compact completeness. The realization of such a unity has kept critics busy for almost two centuries inventing terms that would explain and justify any seeming deviation from such compactness. Incident and episode, as terms that identify respectively the central and peripheral, or essential and adventitious, parts of the action, have served most critics adequately. Although some questioned the propriety of adventitious action and insisted that episode serve as a more integral and less ornamental function,[38] most tacitly accepted the distinction simply by using the terms.[39]

---

[37] "... just as in the other imitative arts one imitation is always of one thing, so in poetry the story, as an imitation of action, must represent one action, a complete whole, with its several incidents so closely connected that the transposal or withdrawal of any one of them will disjoin and dislocate the whole. For that which makes no perceptible difference by its presence or absence is no real part of the whole." From *Introduction to Aristotle, Poetics*, ed. Richard McKeon (New York, 1947), p. 635.

[38] Swedenberg, *Theory of the Epic in England, 1650-1800*. Passages quoted from *Athenian Mercury* (3) p. 220, Dryden (8) p. 222, Gildon (4) pp. 220-221.

[39] Swedenberg, pp. 216-240. Almost all the critics Swedenberg includes in his compendium subscribe to the incident-episode distinction. Kames is perhaps as representative as any of them: "What is the true notion of an episode? Or how is it to be distinguished from what is really a part of the principal action? Every incident that promotes or retards the catastrophe, must be part of the principal action. This clears the nature of an episode; which may be defined: 'An incident connected with the principal action, but which contributes not either to advance or retard it.' The descent of Aeneas into Hell doth not advance or retard the catastrophe; and therefore is an episode. The story of Nisus and Euryalus, producing an alternation in the affairs of the contending parties, is part of the principal action." p. 234.

Some critics sophisticated their discussion by recognizing that episode was related to incident by use of the *in medias res* beginning and the subsequent flashbacks narrated by a character.[40] But even here, the function of narration by a character was never accorded the kind of critical attention worthy of it. Instead, such a flashback was considered as an opportunity for the poet merely to adorn his work with different episodes, to use "the whole world for a stage" and "give him liberty to search thro' the Creation for incidents or adventures for the employment of his Heroes".[41]

*In medias re*s too has been discussed interminably since classical times. Horace, of course, coined the term in the *Ars Poetica*,[42] but Aristotle himself must have been equally concerned with the problem. In the *Poetics*, his famous dictum on unity of action, although it does not mention the *in medias res*, suggests that he must have had something like it in mind when he points to the *Odyssey* (the first Greek epic to use the device) as a poem with an action "that has the kind of unity we are describing".[43] The Italian and French critics of the Renaissance and Neo-Classic ages also discussed in general the problem of *in medias res* without relating it satisfactorily to unity of action or being especially aware of its complexities.[44] As René Bray points out, their commitment

---

That the distinction between the two concepts antedates eighteenth-century criticism is obvious from Spenser's Letter to Ralegh: "But by occasion hereof, many other adventures are intermedled, but rather as *Accidents*, then *intendments*." (Italics mine.) *The Complete Poetical Works of Spenser*, ed., R. E. Dodge (Cambridge, Mass., 1936), p. 137.

[40] In Swedenberg, p. 203, see Broome, "Observations on the Twelfth Book", Pope's Odyssey, III (1725).

[41] "Thus", continues Broome, nullifying by these remarks the value of the insights made earlier, "he was at liberty to ascribe the several dangers of Scylla and Charybdis, of Polypheme and Antipathes to Ulysses, tho' that Heroe had been as unacquainted with those dangers, as Aeneas was in reality with Dido; *the choice of the Episodes being not essential, but arbitrary*." (Italics mine.)

[42] "Ever he hastens to the issue, and hurries his hearer into the story's midst, as if already known, and what he fears he cannot make attractive with his touch he abandons; and so skilfully does he invent, so closely does he blend facts and fiction, that the middle is not discordant with the beginning, nor the end with the middle." From *Horace: Satires, Ars Poetica*, translated by H. Rushton Fairclough (New York, 1926), p. 463.

[43] Aristotle, p. 635.

[44] Jacques Peletier's comments about the problem are typical: "Le commencement doit être modeste, appert et entendible, à l'imitation de la Nature. ... Car l'ordre naturel est de tendre toujours en avancant, et par degres, à une fine heureuse ... le grand Œuvre ne se commence pas à un premier bout: ains a quelque endroit notable des années suivantes". From his *L'Art Poétique*, quoted by W. F. Patterson, *Three Centuries of French Poetic Theory: A Critical History*

to natural time order or artificial time order (*in medias res* with flash-backs) was merely of terminological convenience. They referred to the latter when considering fable (action *plus* episodes) and to the former when considering action (episodes not included).[45] English critics of the eighteenth century, however, were quicker in recognizing the artistry of design in such a structure. Affectively at least, they were aware of the suspense thus generated [46] and the dramatic appropriateness of a narrating character.[47] To be sure, some critics like Gibbon spoke out against the artificial order of *in medias res*,[48] but they were generally in the minority.

---

of the Chief Arts of Poetry in France (1328-1630) (Ann Arbor, 1935), p. 473. Pierre de Ronsard's comments, coming as they do in the preface of his *Franciade*, reveal a poet's predilection for the *in medias res*, but even here his understanding of it, though more unrealized than it is superficial, fails to recognize the extent to which the epic poet exploits a very sophisticated device: "Il faut que l'historien, de poinct en poinct, du commencement jusqu'à la fin, et redevidant le fuzeau au rebours de l'histoire, porte de fureur et d'art ... face que la fin de son ouvrage, per une bonne liaison, se rapporte au commencement. ... [The poet] a pour maxime tres-necessaire en son art de ne suivre jamais pas a pas la verité, mais la vray-semblance et le possible; et sur le possible, et sur que se peut faire, il bastit son ouvrage, laissant la veritable narration aux historiographes, qui poursuivent de fil en esguille, comme on dit en proverbe, leur subject entrepis, du premier commencement jusques à la fin. Au contraire, le poëte bien advise, plein de laborieuse industrie, commence son œuvre par le milieu de l'argument, et quelquefois par la fin; puis il deduit et poursuit si bien son argument par le particulier accident et evenement de la matiere qu'il s'est proposé d'escrire, tantost par personnages par-lans les uns aux autres, tantost par songes, propheties et peintures inserées contre le dos d'une muraille et des harnois, et principalement des boucliers, ou par les dernieres paroles des hommes qui meurent, ou par augures et vol d'oiseaux et phantastiques visions de Dieux et de démons, ou monstrueux langages des chevaus navrez à mort, tellement que le dernier acte de l'ouvrage se cole, se lie et s'en-chaisne si bien et si à propos l'un dedans l'autre, que la fin se rapporte dextrement et artificiellement au premier poinct de l'argument." *Œuvres Complètes de P. de Ronsard*, ed. Prosper Blanchemain (Paris, 1858), pp. 8-20.
[45]   René Bray, *La Formation de la Doctrine Classique en France* (Paris, 1931), p. 195.
[46]   Trapp says: "This method both shortens the Action and exceedingly enter-tains the Reader. The Reasons of which Pleasure is the sudden Surprize of being immediately plunged into the Depth of Action before one is aware; as also of Doubt, and Uncertainty; and afterwards the more agreeable Surprize of having those Doubts cleared, and unravelled." Swedenberg, p. 229.
[47]   Hurd says: "Now these episodical narrations must either proceed from the poet himself, or be imputed to some other who is engaged in the course of the fable; and in either case, must help, indirectly at least, to forward it." Swedenberg, p. 232.
[48]   "When, without any preparation, we are thrown at once into the midst of the subject, unacquainted with the characters or situation of the hero; such a conduct can be productive only of a surprize and perplexity to the reader, which, if they are any beauties, are at least beauties of an inferior species of poetry. Nor is this

In modern times, critical speculation about the device has been
meager, a neglect that is astonishing when one considers the following
points: 1) that the *in medias res* beginning is the most common structural
characteristic of the epic poem and that the poet's sophisticated manipulation of the time-space element probably changed the course of Euro-
pean narrative since the *Odyssey;* 2) that the most spectacular difference
between the *Iliad* and the *Odyssey* (and probably the best argument an
anti-unitarian critic could find against the theory of Homer's authorship
of both poems) is in the utterly dissimilar architectonics of their respective narratives, the former proceeding *ab ovo* and the latter *in medias
res*; 3) that most major epics after the *Odyssey* (including the prose
romantic epics of Heliodorus and his imitator, Sidney) emulate its *in
medias res* structure; [49] 4) that almost every major critic of the epic poem
from Horace to Blackmore recognized the *in medias res* as a commonplace of epic composition.

How then do the classical critical terms here discussed – unity of
action, incident, episode, and *in medias res* – become reconciled to the
concept of voice outlined in the first part of this chapter? The importance of *in medias res* lies not so much in its relationship to the omniscient voice as it does in its *necessary* relationship to that part of the
epic that is narrated with a *restricted* voice, usually of a first person
participant. Once an author has plunged into the middle of an action,
he must sooner or later return to the beginning. But as he has already
committed himself to the omniscient voice, intruding with commentary
and value-judgment (more extensively in the literary epics), narrative

---

all; this very ignorance and perplexity of the reader diminishes the interest of that
part of the poem; for how can we love beauties we are yet ignorant of, or tremble
for misfortunes of which we have a very faint idea?
    When ... the reader, interested in the present misfortunes of the hero, has
little curiosity to inquire into his past ones, it is then the poet chooses to tell
them." Swedenberg, p. 235.
[49]   Even when refusing to use it in *Don Juan*, Byron feels constrained to acknowledge its importance:
    Most epic poets plunge "in medias res"
    (Horace makes this the heroic turnpike road),
    And then your hero tells, whene'er you please,
    What went before – by way of episode,
    While seated after dinner at his ease,
    Beside his mistress in some soft abode,
    Palace, or garden, paradise or cavern,
    Which serves the happy couple for a tavern.
    That is the usual method, but not mine –
    My way is to begin with the beginning ...
                                    (Canto I, vi and vii)

propriety dictates that his return to the beginning be logically and dramatically motivated. An arbitrary disruption of the natural time order with the omniscient narrator skipping hither and yon nullifies any dramatic advantages the artificial order offers to the poet. Exclusive use of the omniscient voice dictates an *ab ovo* and not an *in medias res* structure; and this fact is exemplified by the *ab ovo* epics (*Beowulf*, the *Iliad* and *Gerusalemme Liberata*) that employ generally no voice but the omniscient. But once the *in medias res* is adopted, the exclusive use of the omniscient voice is no longer possible. The poet is forced to return to the flashbacks with a voice that is not omniscient and one whose account of the prerequisite action be dramatically prepared for in the main action itself.

Thus, the easy designation of voice in the epic as omniscient needs to be modified before any exact description of its function can be attempted. Precision of terminology would demand that the omniscience be qualified into a term something like the *delegating omniscient voice*. That is to say, for dramatic reasons already outlined, the omniscient voice delegates large areas of the narration to other voices subordinate to itself. These subordinate voices function as restricted voices *within* an omniscient circumference, taking up the narrative at those strategic moments when a restricted voice would be both necessary and artistically appropriate. A metaphor from modern sound reproduction, though perhaps indecorous, may be useful here. The artistic effect of the delegating omniscient voice in the epic poem is akin to the acoustical channeling of modern stereophonic sound which strategically places speakers of smaller wattage in positions subordinate to the major speaker. The major speaker, at appropriate moments, controls its subordinates by delegating to them sounds that their specialized facilities can more successfully carry, while reserving for itself the bulk of the sound reproduction. The Raphaels and Ulysses of epic literature, then, both of whom are important delegated narrators in their respective poems, function as the "tweeters" and the "woofers" of the epic voice.

This past action thus narrated, although it has been relegated to the level of episode by many critics, actually serves more than a peripheral, or adventitious, or indeed episodic function. Rather, its relationship to the present or future action in the omnisciently narrated area of the poem serves a number of functions which modern critics have never explored in conjunction with the epic but have claimed as the exclusive province of the modern novel. This is not to claim for the epic, of course, the sophisticated techniques of the modern novel. The very nature of the epic's stylized and formalized structure would make any such claim absurd. But it is to claim that within the limits of its structure the epic abounds with sophisticated narrative touches that critics have too long insensitively ignored, touches which, as this study will indicate, are often made possible by the peculiar quality of delegating and delegated omniscient narration.

Among these sophisticated effects is the poet's solving of the problem of exposition. The primary function of the delegated voice, as has already been suggested, is to narrate action dramatically prerequisite to the main action and in point of time previous to it. This kind of exposition naturally allows for a much more compact handling of the poem's own chronological time, a device which Renaissance critics would have called unity of time, but which, for moderns means, less mystically, structural or temporal tightness. The actual time of the *Odyssey*, after all, extends only from the last days of Ulysses' imprisonment on Calypso's island to his slaying of the suitors at Ithaca, a period which an enterprising eighteenth-century critic measured at fifty days,[50] whereas the total narrated time extends to nineteen years.

But obvious as this narrative touch may seem, it occasions some problems which endanger its effective use. The transition point at which the delegated voice takes over from the omniscient, for example, if it is to be artistically successful, demands skillful modulation. Generally speaking, any abrupt switch from one voice to another grates on the reader's ear as seriously as an undeveloped modulation from one key to another in music. Just as the transition from the original key to the dominant chord of the foreign key demands some intricacy of harmonic pattern, so must the transition from the action of the omniscient narration move to the action of the delegated narration with dramatic modulation of some convincingness. Indeed, the shift is sometimes so subtle as to be apparent only after close analysis.

A comparison of the methods used by Homer and Virgil might be fruitful. In the *Odyssey*, the modulation from omniscient narration to Ulysses' narration (Books IX through XII) is handled with consummate skill; whereas the modulation from omniscient narration to Aeneas's narration (Books II and III in the *Aeneid*) is handled less adroitly. In both poems the occasion of a feast leads into the delegated sections (an epic device used by Milton too in *Paradise Lost* [51]). In the *Odyssey*

---

[50] Ogden, "An Introductory Essay on Poetry", *The Revolution*, 1790, p. xviii; quoted by Swedenberg, p. 230.
[51] Book V, lines 395 ff.

Ulysses banquets as guest of the Phaeacians and in the *Aeneid* Aeneas banquets as guest of Dido and Carthaginians. And both poems use as well the epic convention of a bard singing his heroic tales as after-dinner entertainment. But, whereas Iopas – Virgil's bard – sings of "the creation of man and beast, of fire and water" and why "winter suns race on to dip in the ocean",[52] Demodocus – Homer's bard – unaware of the identity of his noble guest, sings of the battle of Troy and the brave Aechaens who met their death there.[53] The contrast between the two transitions is significant. In Virgil's work the presence of the bard represents a mere textural ornament. Aeneas's final rendering of the Troy story is mechanically prepared for in a few lines when love-sick Dido later asks to hear of the fall of Troy and the treachery of the Greeks Ulysses' story of his storm-wracked journey from Troy to the island of Calypso, on the other hand, follows dramatically from the events that preceded it. Demodocus's song so moves Ulysses that he weeps for his departed friends. King Alcinous, noting the emotion, checks the bard and proposes an athletic contest, in which Ulysses triumphs. But toward the close of the festivities, when the blind bard sings of the Greek conquest of Troy and Alcinous notices that Ulysses is again moved to great emotion, the king begs him to relate his adventures and asks with unwitting irony whether he has lost some relative in the war. Thus invited to speak, Ulysses reveals his identity and proceeds to his narration.

In addition to its serving as exposition dramatically conceived, the delegated narration effects an important development in the main action as well. That is to say, just as the story-within-a-story is related organically to what *preceded* it, so is it related organically to what *follows*. When there exists a degree of disproportion between the bulk of the delegated narration and its effect on the subsequent action, the artistic effect of the delegated narration is blunted. In Heliodorus's *Ethiopica,* for example, Calasiris's story is of extremely important expository value (taking up about one-fifth of the work) because it supplies the necessary details about the protagonists: Chariclea and Theagenes. But whatever dramatic effect it might have wielded on the subsequent action is nullified by Heliodorus's choice of audience. Cnemon, a Greek who had helped the protagonists escape from their piratical abductors and who had participated significantly in the action up to the delegated narration, is the only auditor; but his role in the main action after Calasiris's story is negligible. Compared either to the *Aeneid,* in which Aeneas's story

---

[52]   Lines 743-745.
[53]   End of Book VIII.

acts as an aphrodisiac for Dido's affections, or to the *Odyssey*, in which Ulysses' story moves the Phaeacians to compassion and to an offer of naval convoy back to Ithaca, Heliodorus's handling of the delegated voice, in this respect at least, fails.

A more subtle characteristic of the delegated narration is the opportunity it presents for artistic manipulation of suspense, which is served more logically and credibly by the delegated voice than by the omniscient. The withholding of information, or, more exactly, the deliberate patterning of the details of complication in order to contrive an affective uncertainty and anticipation in the auditor, is less appropriate in a narrative controlled exclusively by a voice free of time/space limitations than by a voice restricting itself to the time/space limitation. It is true, of course, that the delegated voice at times claims no more suspense than does the omniscient. Ulysses, in some instances, reveals in advance the outcome of his adventures; and perhaps one might credit Homer with psychological realism for recognizing that a character relating his adventures is more interested in telling the whole story than he is in artificially eliciting a response from his audience. At the same time, however, because suspense is necessarily a by-product of conflict in fiction, it becomes more functional when the narrating voice represents a participating character himself affected by suspense (if only in the telling) than when the voice is omniscient, disembodied and emotionally detached from the action. Moreover, because of the peculiar nature of the *in medius res* structure, the suspense generated functions both forward and backward. Not only is the reader concerned to know the outcome of events as they *will* happen, but also the disposition of events as they *have* happened. Voice in the latter case modulates to the preterite and pluperfect tenses.

In the literary epic, of course, where the action represented is of common knowledge to the audience, the backward and forward suspense is concerned not so much with the *what* as with the details of *how*. Virgil's Roman audience knew of the Trojan horse, but they did not know precisely how or why a hideous artifact large enough to contain a host of Greek soldiers was dragged into the city. The delegated voice of Aeneas in Book II tells them in suspenseful detail both how and why. On the other hand, suspense in the romantic epic, because that poem is less derivative and more inventive, abounds both in the *what* and the *how* of the conflict, both in present and past action. Sidney's audience were concerned not only about Musidorus's attempts to rescue Pyrocles from the pirates in the first book of the *Arcadia* but also what the two

men were doing washed up and near the shore in the first place. The
delegated voices of Musidorus and Pyrocles near the middle of the first
book answer to both the active and retroactive suspense thus generated.

Yet, these immediate dramatic relationships of the delegated narration
to the main action represent, despite their artistry, the surface narrative
strokes of a skilled poet. They are enlisted here, among other reasons, in
order to argue against the stock eighteenth-century concept of episode
as ornament, the facile insistence that "the true criterion of the propriety
of an epic episode is the possibility of the reader's passing it over without
breaking, in the least degree, the chain of the narrative".[54] But the very
physical position of the delegated narration within the larger circumference of the omniscient narration offers the epic poet a number of
artistic opportunities which go beyond the mere dramatic manipulation
of exposition and suspense. First of all, it offers the poet an excellent
opportunity to lay aside temporarily the explicit, over-drawn style of
characterization that results necessarily from an omniscient voice. By
making use of the restricted voice, he brings to the epic not only the
obvious dramatic advantages of a character telling his own story but he
is also able to complement the revelations of omniscient characterization
with the revelations of restricted characterization. It is as if a person who
has been talked about by others (in this case, of course, the "others" is
the all-knowing voice) suddenly comes upon the scene and reveals himself by the vehicle of his own words. Sometimes the revelations thus
achieved are only literally complementary to the testimony of the earlier
voice, but sometimes they are ironically complementary, producing a
dramatic situation which tends to the sophisticated and the indirect. In
Sidney's *New Arcadia*, for example, the revelations by the princes about
their own heroic adventures before the *in medias res* beginning literally
corroborate the omniscient voice's previous judgment that Pyrocles ("a
Mars's heart in a Cupid's body") is more amorously inclined than
Musidorus, despite the unquestioned military heroism of them both and
Musidorus's eventual romancing of Pamela. But in the same work
Kalander's fond and ingenuous remarks about the angelic virtue of his
two royal nieces – the object of the princes' attention – are ironically
overstated when the reader compares their all too human (and feminine)
qualities, as the omniscient voice sketches them, with Kalander's account. Naturally, the final effect of restricted character revelation will
act to corroborate the "telling" of the omniscient voice. Whether the

---

[54]   Drake, *Literary Hours*, quoted by Swedenberg, p. 240.

corroboration is literal or ironic will not change the irrefutable testimony of the omniscient voice. Irrefutable it must be because it is omniscient. Thus, even the most sophisticated use of voice in the epic would seldom result in a question mark about character, the kind of result one finds in *The Ring and the Book* where the testimonies of many restricted voices are juxtaposed. The epic may use a variety of restricted voices or a single restricted voice (the tendency to variety accentuated by the intention of the romantic epic and de-emphasized by the intention of the literary epic), but in either case the final result corroborates the omniscient voice's testimony by means of fuller and more realistic characterization.

In addition to serving the narrative devices of exposition, suspense, and characterization, the delegated narration often reflects significantly the theme of the main action. Sometimes the theme is reflected simply (as a straight mirror reflects simply), sometimes with partial distortion (as a convex mirror both magnifies and shrinks different parts of the same image). But however simple or inverted the reflection, it serves brilliantly as a device of dramatic and thematic foreshadowing. When this device operates as a simple parallel, it results in uncomplicated architectonic symmetry, the same kind of symmetry for its own sake that leads to the repetition of circles, squares, or other geometric designs in the plastic arts and to leitmotifs in music. Fradubio's story of his deception at the hands of Fidessa and the unhappy consequences there-of in Book I of *The Faerie Queene*, for example, foreshadow without distortion Red Cross Knight's allegorical plight with the same woman (Duessa). Less simple a device of foreshadowing is Menalaus's account in Book III of the *Odyssey* of his stormy, interminable voyage from Troy back to Sparta. Coming as it does early in the poem, it does look forward by simple parallelism to Ulysses' own successful though delayed journey from Troy to Ithaca. But this restricted narration foreshadows with an ironic difference, for the pitifully domestic peace that is granted to the heroic cuckold and the adulterous Helen, both oblivious to the Trojan blood-letting that made their reunion possible, is significantly different from the exercise in carnage that the battle-weary Ulysses is once again forced to practice before his reunion with the faithful Penelope becomes possible.

Irony in all its manifestations – verbal, dramatic and situational – enters spectacularly in these episodes narrated by the restricted voice. By his oblivious silence about his complicity in the deaths of thousands of Greek and Trojan heroes, for example, Menelaus convicts himself and his wife more completely than any omnisciently voiced accusation could have succeeded in accomplishing. The omniscient narrator, because he is either divine or inspired to truthful utterance by divinity, must largely reveal himself in explicit statement: he cannot for very long conceal his attitudes without somehow giving up his omniscience. Paradox may lend itself to omniscient narration – as it does in the Gospels – but not irony. An unreliable omniscient narrator – however minimal his unreliability – would clearly be a contradiction in terms. Yet it is inconceivable that the epic poet, as his society's consummate practitioner of human speech, would not have felt the need for ironic utterance. Certainly in his own un-epical life, the opportunities for ironic commentary – both as speaker and listener – would never have been denied him. Nor is it conceivable that by the tyranny of poetic tradition he would have denied himself ironic utterance in that most lofty of literary enterprises – the epic poem. Man cannot stand too much oracle. It is here, therefore, in the ironic parallels of the episodes, that the restricted human voice impinges most stridently upon the omniscient. It is only here that crafty Ulysses, stolid Menelaus and garrulous Nestor can reveal to us the peculiar humanity that is their special glory.

II. THE CLASSICAL EXEMPLUM

1

The three species of epic referred to in the last chapter will be represented in this study by the works of Homer, Sidney, Milton and Spenser.[1] My decision to devote a chapter to the *Odyssey* is prompted by the fact that I judge it to be the example *par excellence* of the delegating omniscient voice and that its structure influenced most fully the great English epics. My decision to limit the discussion of the English epics to the *New Arcadia, Paradise Lost* and *The Faerie Queene* is prompted by the obvious judgment that these are the best epic offerings in English literature. The fact that they happen to have been produced within one hundred years of each other is of no special significance in this study. I have not chosen them because they are Renaissance epics; rather, I have chosen them because they are the best epics. I leave critical discussion of the later English epics – curiosities like Blackmore's *King Arthur* and Southey's *Joan of Arc* – to scholars with stronger constitutions.[2] I do not include *Beowulf*, despite its great merits, because it is totally outside the tradition that leads from Homer and also because it is not an *in medias res* epic. The genius of its poet received its inspiration from a tradition only remotely related to the one I will sketch here.

2

Any responsible criticism of the Greek epic must be prefaced with a discussion of certain assumptions that have not yet been universally accepted by the world of scholarship. These assumptions are: 1) The *Iliad* and the *Odyssey* were written each by a single poet. The author of

---

[1] Homer will represent the heroic poem, Sidney and Spenser the romantic epic, and Milton the literary epic.
[2] See Peter Hagin, *The Epic Hero and the Decline of Epic Poetry* (Bern, 1964) and Brian Wilkie, *Romantic Poets and Epic Tradition* (Madison, 1965).

the *Iliad* may not have been the same man as the author of the *Odyssey,*
but each work is the product of a single artist. This kind of unitarian
assumption absolutely precludes the possibility that the poems, in the
form in which they have survived, represent a kind of catalogue of epic
lays. 2) The *Iliad* and the *Odyssey* are the products of an oral formulaic
system of epic composition that makes possible a unitarian theory of
authorship. To agree with Wolf – that the extraordinary length of these
poems would have made oral composition by a single poet impossible –
would render literary criticism of these poems meaningless. But now that
the field work of men like Milman Parry and Albert Lord has restored
scholarly confidence in the theory of unitarian composition,[3] literary
criticism of Homer becomes possible again. 3) The genius of Homer is
not incompatible with the oral formulaic system of epic composition.
Rather the oral formulaic poet must be judged within the limitations of
his own medium. The oral tradition does, in some ways, limit the narrative art of an epic singer, but in many ways it offers him larger stylistic
building blocks with which to proceed. As Whitman points out:

Oral poetry is neither primitive nor mechanical, nor does its traditional
nature preclude the play of genius. Its methods may differ to a degree from
those of written literature, and therefore Homer's greatness will not be
found in imagined departures from oral technique, any more than Shakespeare's can be discovered by trying to envision those moments when he
threw away his quill and chanted his verses aloud. A poet's native medium
is his best artistic device. In seeking Homer's original genius, we must not
seek the newly turned phrase, the non-formulaic line, or even the character
who . . . did not exist in previous tradition. It is not outside tradition that
Homer has triumphed, but within it.[4]

3

With these assumptions removed from the arena of dispute and with the
single authorship of the *Iliad* and *Odyssey* back in favor, literary criticism of Homer becomes possible again. Two considerations will be
paramount in the following analysis, considerations which have been
only roughly mapped out in the previous chapter. The first is that the
breadth of omniscient voice in an epic is determined by the particular
species of epic that the voice is "subject to". Conditioned by the
exigencies of oral recitation, for example, the omniscient voice of the
heroic poem refrains from the kind of incidental, extra-narrative activity

---

[3] For a review of this whole controversy, see Cedric H. Whitman, *Homer and
the Heroic Tradition*, Chapter I.
[4] Whitman, p. 6.

common to the literary and romantic epic. One finds few philosophical digressions, lyrical interludes, and political and teleological prophecies in the heroic poem. The second consideration, more important and of central significance throughout the rest of this study, is that in epics of *in medias res* structure the omniscient voice delegates to another, restricted voice that part of the total narrative that precedes in time the events of the *in medias res* beginning and delegates it in a way that indicates the poet's real awareness of the narrative artistry of restricted voice. Happily, the classical epic affords excellent examples of both considerations, especially the latter.

Schiller in his famous definition of epic – that it is "in style objective ... [narrating] habitually without interposition by images visual, auditory, motor", that its "method is to suggest heroic life by its physical sensations, to make the characters, as Aristotle says, reveal themselves" [5] – misunderstands to a certain extent the function of the omniscient voice. Certainly his insistence that Homer and Shakespeare are as invisible behind their material as the Creator behind his universe applies to Shakespeare with more accuracy than it does to Homer. The careful reader of the Homeric poems is constantly aware of the existence of the author: by his reference to the Muses, by subjective explanation of events or causes that cannot be related with complete objectivity, by the poet's explicit reaction, favorable or unfavorable, to an event he is narrating, at times even by the poet's direct address to the character in the story who is at the moment dramatically important. As Bassett points out:

We must remember the difference between the epic poem and the simple account of facts. The child or the primitive savage is purely objective in his report of a highly emotional incident. It is only by repeated questioning that he yields the details from which the scene may be reconstructed in the imagination. The oral epic poet must anticipate such questions in the mind of his audience; he must furnish the details along with the facts, and he must do this in such a way as both to facilitate the imaginative construction of the scene and to heighten its emotional effect. Hence any tale worthy of the name cannot be by any means purely objective.[6]

What part of the narrative in Homer transcends the limitations of the "purely objective"? Or in terms to which this study is addressed, where does the main impact of the omniscient narration make itself felt in Homer? The most obvious answer, of course, is present in Homer's

---

[5] Quoted in Samuel E. Bassett, *The Poetry of Homer* (Berkeley, 1938), p. 81.
[6] Bassett, p. 83.

panoramic vision of his own world. When he is not delegating omniscience to a narrating character, his point of view leads from a position that makes everything in time and place open to himself, from the splendor of Zeus's court to the squalor of Eumaeus's cave, from the recesses of Hera's Zeus-seducing mind to the erratic behavior of Eurycleia's memory. Apart from the panoramic view peculiar to this kind of narration, however, Homer's omniscience reveals itself precisely in those subjective areas where Schiller insisted the "naive" epic author never moved, in the area of interposition, intrusion, non-dramatic value-judgment. Bassett has pointed to slight but significant examples of this.[7] More obvious examples would include: 1) the poet's open revelation of the outcome of some encounter (at Patroclus's request to Achilles that his chief allow him to enter the battle, the poet interrupts with: "He knew not what he was asking, nor that he was suing for his own destruction" [8]; 2) the poet's prayer to the Muses that they supply the correct details of historical information that he is about to relate ("Tell me now, O Muses . . . who was the first of the Argives to bear away blood-stained spoils after Neptune . . . had turned the fortune of war?"); 3) the poet's undramatic appraisal of a situation wedged into his otherwise objective account of the action (about the exchange of armor that took place at the Glaucus-Diomede truce, the poet says: "But the son of Saturn made Glaucus take leave of his wits, for he exchanged golden armour for bronze, the worth of a hundred head of cattle for the worth of nine" [9]; 4) the poet's direct second-person address to a character at the moment involved in the action (Menelaus, Melanippus, Patroclus and Appolo are so addressed in the *Iliad*, Eumaeus in the *Odyssey*).

Yet, when one compares Homer to Virgil by testing in their epics the ratio of objective to subjective elements, one finds a quality of omniscience in the former that is remarkably more confined. Partially, perhaps chiefly, this limitation is due to the medium, to the species of epic poem that each was composing. In the oral epic, the poet's tone is *literally* present: in his, or the rhapsode's, voice, his delivery, his very physical presence. The degree of explicitness necessary to the audience's appreciation of the story does not always need to be supplied by the narrated word. Approbation or disapprobation, tonal subtlety, irony can be

---

[7]   Bassett, p. 87.
[8]   *The Iliad of Homer and the Odyssey*, translated by Samuel Butler, Great Books of the Western World, Vol. 4 (Chicago, 1948), Book XVI, l. 46, p. 112. All future references to the *Iliad* and *Odyssey* will be to this volume.
[9]   VI, 232.

supplied by a gesture, a vocal inflection, even a raised eyebrow. The literary poet has no such "on-the-spot" advantage. He is totally cut off from his audience and, as C. S. Lewis points out, must simulate the ritualistic occasion of the recited epic by means of a heightened style. In the literary epic "there are no external aids to solemnity which the Primary [heroic] poem enjoyed. . . . The Virgilian and Miltonic style is there to compensate for – to counteract – the privacy and informality of silent reading in a man's study." [10]

How does this heightened style affect the degree of omniscience in an epic? If the above thesis is correct in stating that the literary poet must compensate tonally for his physical absence from the audience, then more of him*self* – by intrusions if necessary – must find its way into the poem. With three poetic manners operating in any epic – the objective narration proper, the dramatically imitative (dialogue), and the subjec- tively explanatory – any proportionate increase in the latter will neces- sarily result in a decrease of the first two. But any decrease in dialogue and in objective narration – the agents of restriction in an omniscient structure – will extend the breadth of omniscience considerably. Bassett has estimated that the Homeric poems contain one-fifth objective narra tion, three-fifths dialogue or speeches, and one-fifth subjective explana- tion. Although statistics are not available for the *Aeneid,* a close reading should reveal considerably fewer speeches and considerably less inclina- tion to use direct discourse. A comparison of the first books of the *Odyssey* and the *Aeneid,* for example, tends to indicate the general ratio of direct discourse to narrative. Of the 440 lines in the first book of the *Odyssey,* 298 represent direct discourse. Of the 756 lines in the first book of the *Aeneid,* only 319 represent direct discourse. 67 per cent of the lines of the *Odyssey* (assuming these proportions could be extended throughout the epic) is utilized for direct dramatic imitation; only 42 per cent of the *Aeneid,* however, is so utilized.

But the number of speeches is only as significant as their quality and function. From Homer's extensive use of speeches that by themselves reveal the character of the speaker we recognize a self-imposed limitation on his omniscient voice. Examples can be multiplied, but one will suffice here. The omniscient characterization of Nestor as an old man, wise in council, is corroborated in Nestor's own speeches, but in a way that brings more truth and more of the human being to his character than any series of epithets could ever hope to accomplish. For from Nestor's

[10]   *A Preface to Paradise Lost,* pp. 40-41.

speeches we learn not only that he is an old man, wise in council, but also that he is a garrulous old man who often reminisces about his youth and former glory at most improbable times. In Book XI of the *Iliad*, when Achilles sends Patroclus in the heat of battle to inquire of Nestor the identity of the wounded man removed from the field, Nestor, stung by the thought of Achilles' refusal to fight, answers peevishly: "Why should Achilles care...? Our most valiant chieftains lie disabled"; whereupon he lists those who have been wounded in battle and ends with a lament for his own lack of strength. If the speech had ended there, it would have characterized Nestor closely, but not precisely enough. Instead, Homer allows Nestor to continue speaking, and what he relates, considering the circumstances, turns out to be an absurdly lengthy and unnecessarily detailed story of an incident in his own youth when he battled the men of Elis. Whitman suggests that speeches of this kind objectify the inner state of a character whose creator had not yet the opportunity to use the "stream-of-consciousness" technique,[11] and that the seeming incongruity of a speech like Eurycleia's in the *Odyssey*, flashing back 76 lines between her recognition of Ulysses' scar and her gesture of joyous surprise, is simply a dramatization of her mental image. Be that as it may, whether we interpret Nestor's utterances as an example of mental image or an actual speech (and I would incline to the latter in Nestor's case), the result of characterization by the technique of personal exposure is the same. We know more about Nestor because Homer has allowed Nestor to speak of himself in a peculiarly revealing way than we could have known by a detached, omniscient characterization or by a different kind of speech, one that merely tends to put quotes around lines which, with a change of the personal pronoun, could just as easily have been spoken by the poet himself.

Homer's self-imposed limitation on his omniscient narration reveals itself in still another way in the *Iliad*. It is common, as I have just pointed out, for Homer's heroes to reveal details about their characters that the omniscient voice simply could not reach. A less common, but perhaps more skillful method of restricted characterization, is Homer's way of revealing the character of his heroes by what *other* people say. The most impressive example occurs in Book III of the *Iliad* just before the single combat between Paris and Menelaus. At this point in the poem, the Greek *dramatis personae* had not been "formally" introduced. Except for Agamemnon and Achilles in their quarrel, Homer had merely scattered hints about the other characters. As Helen is summoned to the wall to view the battle, Priam calls her to his side to tell him the names of those heroes who by their noble bearing seem to stand out from the rest. Helen then names Agamemnon, Ulysses, Ajax, and Idomeneus, drawing a short character sketch of each. What Homer has done here, it seems, is to allow some of his heroes to be formally introduced without offending by familiarity his Greek audience, who obviously would have been as familiar with their heroes as an American audience would be with George Washington. To have introduced them omnisciently would have involved with no real purpose the repetition of epithets like "crafty" Ulysses. The Greek audience knew all about "crafty" Ulysses. But to allow Helen, whose fate is ironically entangled with the heroes she describes, to introduce them to Priam, who has never met them but who will suffer much from them in the near future, is to succeed in setting up a *dramatis personae* of ironic anticipation.

Two fairly lengthy interpolated stories, one told by Glaucus to Diomede in Book VI and the other by Phoenix to Achilles in Book IX further suggest Homer's self-imposed limitation on his omniscient voice and, precociously, his awareness of the function of a narrating character. At first glance, the Phoenix story seems to be more closely related to the main action, paralleling in its account of the recalcitrant Meleager, who refuses out of anger to do battle with Auretes, Achilles' own refusal to do battle against the Trojans. But the parallel is not subtle, Phoenix himself pointing out the relationship as a moral exemplum for Achilles. The other story serves no parallel function but rather identifies the families of Glaucus and Diomede as closely related in ancient friendships and, as Whitman points out, "illustrates the maintenance of contact between the Aechaens overseas [at Troy] and the old families at home".[12] As such the story functions as a peace maker for two warriors who refuse to fight each other when they hear it, as a kind of ironic reminder that the war in which thousands of their compatriots are similarly involved and to some extent related by blood is totally futile. Homer's hatred for war, despite its heroic celebration in the *Iliad*, reveals itself dramatically, and not declamatorily, here.

It is not the purpose of this chapter to determine the extent to which Virgil places a self-imposed limitation on his omniscient voice in the *Aeneid*; but one cannot help feeling that in contrast to Homer's incipient sense of restricted characterization in the *Iliad* Virgil remains fixed on

12   Whitman, p. 39.

the level of omniscient characterization. The impression often gained is that when Virgil's characters are speaking the omniscient voice has not relinquished its control over them but uses them as a mouthpiece, rhetorical and declamatory. And in Virgil's peculiar use of the Muse this impression is strengthened. Not only is Virgil's invocation to the Muse more frequent than Homer's, but it is also more indiscriminate. That is, whenever Virgil recognizes the need for a solemn heightening of style, whether the need should come at a moment of extended description, of historical exposition, or of a causal connection between events, he does not hesitate to call upon her. Moreover, his invocation pleads that the Muse employ the poet as her mouthpiece, in the Heliconian sense. "Come, Muse of Love", Virgil writes (at a moment of particularly undramatic exposition in Book VII), "let me rehearse the kings, the phase of History, and the conditions that reigned in antique Latium/ When first that expedition arrived upon the beaches of Italy. . . . *Speak through me, then, Spirit of Song!*" [13] Whether Virgil uses this kind of invocation as a genuine heart-felt prayer or as a heightened rhetorical device to simulate the occasion of the Homeric epic matters not at all. If the poet thinks he is the human instrument of the divine singer, then he has at least convinced himself that the divine view is his view. If, on the other hand, the poet is merely affecting inspiration, he has at least committed himself dramatically to the omniscient view of the divine inspirer. The final effect of either possibility remains the same. The breadth of omniscience becomes necessarily extended.

In Homer, the invocation to the Muse is not Heliconian, but Olympian. "Homer's Muses do not dwell in the Pierian valley, but on Olympus. They are in no wise chthonian; their power is not mysterious and their gift is not transcendental. The Muse is the daughter of Zeus, whose voice is authority. . . . the authentic Voice of the Past." [14] Contrary to the common assumption that in Homer the poet is the spokesman of the Muse, then, it would seem that he is more of a "Pelagian" poet, that he calls for divine help only to validate historically his version of the past:

The poet's own tale of the long-vanished past has the supreme sanction for its veracity. The brief appeal to the Muse in the proems makes the audience hear, as it were, the voice of one who was present, the daughter of Zeus, "who above all others bringeth true tidings to men." How better could the

---

[13] *The Aeneid of Virgil*, translated by C. Day Lewis (New York, 1953), p. 157 (italics mine).
[14] Bassett, p. 31.

hearer be made to feel – all unconsciously – that he was to view with the eye of the imagination the reincarnation of great human lives? [15]

4

Lest the preceding discussion (whose purpose it was to indicate the significant differences between omniscient voice in the literary epic and omniscient voice in the heroic poem) suggest that the *Iliad* and the *Odyssey* utilize equally the narrative advantages of restricted voice, I must make clear now that the quality of restriction in the *Iliad* is different in kind from the quality of restriction in the *Odyssey* and that the differences are intimately related to the structural problem of *in medias res*. To point to both the *Iliad* and the *Odyssey* as examples of poems beginning *in medias res* is to misunderstand the essential meaning of the term by confusing the total occasion of an epic with its actual narrative boundaries. The *total* setting of the *Iliad* can be considered to be the Trojan War, which began with Paris's abduction of Helen and ended with the sack of Troy. When the reader keeps this *terminus a quo* and *terminus ad quem* in mind, and he remembers that the first book of the *Iliad* begins with the disastrous quarrel between Achilles and Agamemnon, he assumes that the poet has plunged in *medias res* by beginning his story late in the war. The actual *terminus a quo* and *terminus ad quem* of the *Iliad*, the setting dictated by the plot of the narrative itself, is much more limited however. Although the reader may interpret the quarrel, in the larger context of the war, as coming *in medias res*, he must recognize that in the limited context of the poem the quarrel occurs precisely at the beginning. What the reader and careless critic have done, therefore, is to confuse the term *in medias res* with *in media belli*. The two terms are certainly not synonymous. One may disagree with C. S. Lewis that the Trojan War is not the subject of the *Iliad,* that it is "merely the background of a purely personal story – that of Achilles' wrath, suffering, repentance and killing of Hector",[16] but one cannot disagree about the temporal confines of the work. The killing of Hector may well symbolize the eventual destruction of Troy, but in point of actual chronology in the *Iliad* the topless towers have not yet begun to burn. If one were to label temporally the order of incidents in the *Iliad*, he would discover a perfectly untampered chronology proceeding from the beginning – the quarrel – to the end – Hector's funeral.

The *terminus a quo* of the *Odyssey* – Ulysses' departure from Troy –

[15] P. 32.
[16] *Preface to Paradise Lost*, p. 28.

does not, however, come at the actual beginning. The departure itself is
not spoken of until Book III in Nestor's story, and its details are not
explored until Book IX where Ulysses begins his great narration. The epic
begins, in terms of *narrated* beginning, where Telemachus decides to
make search for his father, who, as we discover in Book V, is imprisoned on Calypso's island. (I discount here, of course, the "argument"
of Book I which reveals all this information before the action com-
mences.) The interim details from the *terminus a quo* of the poem to the
narrated beginning of the poem thus are supplied later by one major
and two minor narrating characters to whom the poet delegates his story.

Homer's entirely different commitments to temporal structure in the
Iliad and the *Odyssey*, as I have briefly pointed out already, are responsible for the entirely different kinds of voice operating in the two
poems. Voice in the *Iliad* may be described as a modified omniscience
working with the structure of temporal contiguity; voice in the *Odyssey*
may be described as an omniscience which, for purposes of narrating the
prerequisite action, delegates its function to one or more restricted
voices.

Whitman, in his enlightening discussion of structural design in the
Iliad, has offered an architectonic theory that can be utilized here both
as a point of reference and a point of departure. Suggesting that the
structure of the *Iliad* can be seen as a literary counterpart of Greek
geometric vase design and proving that the age of geometric vase design
coincided with the time of Homer, Whitman proceeds to see the *Iliad* as
an incredibly balanced poem, "a schematicized pattern rationally worked
out and altogether consistent with the observable artistic practices of the
Geometric Age".[17]

The principles of circularity, including concentricity, or framing by balanced similarity and antithesis, is one of the chief dynamic forces under-
lying the symmetry of Geometric vase design. In the *Iliad,* the old device
of hysteron proteron has been expanded into a vast scheme far transcending
any mere mnemonic purpose, a scheme purely and even abstractly architectonic. Not only are certain whole books of the poem arranged in self-
reversing or balancing designs, but the poem as a whole is, in a way, an
enormous hysteron proteron, in which books balance books and scenes
balance scenes by similarity or antithesis, with amazing virtuosity.[18]

To do justice to Whitman's theory, I shall reproduce here one example
of what he means by structural hysteron proteron. Bowra had recognized

[17]   Whitman, p. 250.
[18]   P. 255.

the antithetical relationships of the first book with the last, the epic beginning "with an uncontrolled scene of wrath and [ending] with the appeasing of wrath in reconciliation".[19] But Whitman's critical contribution is in seeing the antithesis working within the incidents of the books themselves.[20]

BOOK I

1. Plague and funerals
2. Quarrel and seizure of Briseis
3. Thetis and Achilles (appeal to Zeus)
   Journey to Chrysa
4. Thetis and Zeus (adoption of Achilles' cause)
5. Quarrel on Olympus

BOOK XXIV

5. Quarrel on Olympus
4. Thetis and Zeus (modification of hero's cause)
3. Thetis and Achilles (message from Zeus)
   Journey of Priam
2. Reconciliation and restitution (of Hector's body)
1. Funeral of Hector

Such a geometric design makes impossible, and this is my point in dwelling on Whitman's theory, any manipulation of normal temporal pattern. That is to say, if Books I, II, III, IV function in reverse balance to Books XXIV, XXIII, XXII, XXI, the reversal can only make sense in terms of temporal *order*. And because the contiguous chronology of the *Iliad* needs no significant exposition (the *terminus a quo* coinciding with the narrated beginning), the poem contains no inherent obstacles to a geometric ordering of its large structure. Moreover, there exists a natural, almost ineffable, affinity between the omniscient voice and this kind of structural pattern. Because the omniscient voice in the *Iliad* never delegates or "gives away" its function, its control over the structure is first-hand and proximate, foreseeing the end while it describes the beginning. It is true that when the omniscient voice yields its function to a restricted voice it is in fact *assuming* limited narration while all the time controlling and ordering as it did in an exclusively omniscient narration. But, at the same time, by delegating a significant segment of

---

[19]   C. M. Bowra, *Tradition and Design in the Iliad* (Oxford, 1930), p. 16.
[20]   Whitman charts the entire plot in the pull-out sheet in the back cover.

the narration, as in the *Odyssey*, the omniscient voice foresakes the immediate, geometric control that it wields while functioning alone. If one can believe with Keats and Hazlitt that the great artist becomes the thing he creates, that his negative capability must necessarily result in a sympathetic identification with his creation, then in a very real sense, the omniscient voice, having one delegated its authority, can no longer control in quite the same way. Having passed its function to another, it must honor for the moment the autonomous voice of the subordinate.

Thus, what becomes possible by way of geometric structure with a work controlled entirely by an omniscient voice is not possible in a work controlled by both omniscient and restricted voices. And thus, the kind of geometric balance one finds in the *Iliad* cannot, because of the very nature of the narrating voices, be repeated in the *Odyssey*. Furthermore, the kind of balance intended in the *Odyssey* is not the balance of geometric structure but rather the balance of tones – an ironic counterpointing of attitudes. And since irony works best when functioning within the range of restricted narration (when the voice, that is, is not directly conscious of the irony), the *Odyssey* with its restricted voice exploits irony to the fullest. A discussion of these ironic balances will occupy the next section. Suffice it to repeat here that whereas Homer in the *Iliad* exhibited an artistry of geometric architectonics made possible by his exclusive use of the omniscient voice (albeit a modified one), in the *Odyssey* his artistic experimentation with restricted voice led him away from formal geometric design and resulted in an entirely different kind of balance.

5

The *Odyssey* is without a doubt the best example in classical literature of the omniscient voice delegating artistically to subordinate voices large areas of the narration. Unlike Virgil, who awkwardly uses the device of the delegated narrator for only two books early in his epic (II and III) and then proceeds to an uninterrupted, completely omniscient and chronological narration of Aeneas's adventures, Homer in the *Odyssey* uses the restricted voice fully in four books and partially in two more, manipulating the elements of time and space with infinitely more skill than his Roman imitator.

Most commentators have paid little *critical* attention to the fact that the account of Ulysses' wanderings are never related by the omniscient voice but are narrated exclusively by Ulysses himself. Certainly, every critic has recognized that the entire length of Books IX, X, XI and XII is enclosed in editorial quotation marks, but most have neglected to relate this fact to the intention of the whole.

That Homer was acutely sensitive to the demands and to the dramatic advantages of the restricted voice (never allowing the restricted narration to become a mere mouthpiece for the omniscient but respecting always the former's autonomy) can be proved by a close reading of the poem. In the first place, the restricted voice is always faithful to the limitations of its restricted knowledge, never reporting events that it could not itself have known, never assuming for a moment an omniscient timbre. Examples of this kind of narrative "epistemology" are numerous, but three will suffice. When Ulysses relates his Circe adventure to the Phaeacians in Book X, he explains that a company of his men led by Eurylochus was chosen to explore Circe's island, his own company having been left behind to guard the ships. The next lines describe the "porcine" fate of the men when they reached Circe's house, an event that Ulysses, back at the ships, could not have known. However, by including in Ulysses' account of the adventure, the simple detail of Eurylochus suspecting mischief, staying outside and reporting back to Ulysses the sad fate of his comrades, Homer succeeds in scrupulously respecting the limitations of the restricted voice. Again, at the end of Book XII when Ulysses describes the divine anger at his crew's slaying of the sun cattle, the account includes what Lampetie reported to Hyperion, what Hyperion complained of to Jove, and finally how Jove promised divine punishment for the sin. Obviously, Ulysses' knowledge could not have extended to the divine councils, and for the moment this episode reads like a restricted narration in which the limitations of knowledge in restricted voice have been forgotten. But a few lines later, Ulysses reports: "I was told all this by Calypso, who said she had heard it from the mouth of Mercury." [21]

The most sophisticated example of this kind of awareness occurs in the voyage-to-the-underworld episode in Book XI. Ulysses meets, among others, his old chieftain Agamemnon, who after much lamentation reveals the circumstances of his death at the hands of Aegisthus and inquires solicitously after his own son, Orestes. Ulysses' reply – "why do you ask me? I do not know whether your son is alive or dead, and it is not right to talk when one does not know" – is not only faithful to the obvious limitations of his own knowledge under the circumstances, but also observes an extraordinary respect for the fact of manipulated time

[21]   XII, 389.

in the poem. By Ulysses' own calculations, he spent the last seven years of his ten-year voyage imprisoned on Calypso's island. His wanderings, reported in Books IX through XII, would necessarily have taken place in the first three years. From Nestor's account of the voyage back from Troy we learn that Menelaus returned home eight years after his departure from the sacked city: and his return coincided exactly with the day that Orestes was celebrating the funerals of Aegisthus and Clytemnestra. Therefore, although Orestes' vengeance in the manipulated chronology of the narrative had already been reported *before* Ulysses' encounter with Agamemnon,[22] in point of *real* time Ulysses in Book XI could not in fact have known of Orestes' vengeance, first because he had no opportunity to know, but, more significantly, because the event had not yet taken place. At the point, of course, at which Ulysses is *telling* the story – presumably the tenth year of his voyages – Orestes' vengeance had already been two years old, but because Ulysses, detained as he was on Calypso's island at the time of the vengeance, could not have known of Orestes' act, he does not report it to the Phaeacians even in what might have been an aside.

The real chronology would look like this: a) second year – Ulysses meets Agamemnon in Hades, does not know the fate of Orestes; b) eighth year – Orestes avenges his father's murder by killing Aegisthus and Clytemnestra; c) tenth year – Ulysses tells his version of the meeting in Hades to the Phaeacians. The manipulated order of narration, however, is: b, c, a – with b narrated twice, once by Nestor in Book III and again by Menelaus in Book IV. Ulysses's expression of his ignorance, therefore, both circumstantially and chronologically true, is remarkable when one realizes that the occasion for chronological error in an oral epic complicated by manipulated time would have been more than likely.

But the poet's fidelity to the knowledge of his restricted voice is not the only indication of artistic awareness of the restricted narration. It would be folly, of course, to expect that Homer would tailor the style of his restricted narration to the character of his narrator. The physical limitations of an oral formulaic style would have made such a modern narrative device almost impossible. Yet, if we examine certain characteristics of the style of the omniscient voice and that of the restricted, we find at least one significant difference – the use of epic simile. Such a device would function as the natural tool of the omniscient narration.

[22]   Nestor had informed Telemachus of this fact in Book III.

With its complex parallelism and formal syntax, with its recognition of artificial resemblances between often dissimilar things, the epic simile is well suited to the timbre of the omniscient voice. Such a device used repeatedly either in dialogue or in the delegated narration, however, would militate against the more limited observation of the restricted voice.

Bowra has pointed out that the *Odyssey* has far fewer similes than the *Iliad* because it is Homer's practice to use the simile more often in battle scenes which, unrelieved by variation, would tend to become monotonous.[23] As correct as this insight may be, he neglects to mention that Homer uses the full-blown epic simile almost exclusively when he is speaking in his own voice with omniscient formality. When on those few occasions that the simile is used within dialogue, he usually modifies its formal syntax to suit the exigencies of speech. Of the 144 fully developed similes in the *Iliad*, for example, three are spoken by characters and the rest by the omniscient author. Of the eleven similes in the *Odyssey* used in dialogue, only four make use of the formal syntax of the epic simile. The other seven are clearly modified and shortened syntactically to fit into the more regular patterns of normal speech. Moreover, the proportion of formal epic similes from the *Iliad* to the *Odyssey* – 144 in the former, 23 in the latter – suggests more than the poet's predilection for similes in the battle scenes. It suggests too that because the *Iliad* contains no significant restricted narration, the epic simile would fit more naturally into its omnisciently narrated style. And because the frequency of epic simile seems to occur in inverse proportion to the amount of restricted narration, the *Odyssey* would logically show a more limited use of the device.

Homer's artistic awareness of the function of restricted voice in the *Odyssey* extends beyond his fidelity to the epistemology of his narrator and his judicious use of the epic simile. It takes into account the very obvious but the very often neglected fact that the audience of an internal narrator is quite different from the audience whom the omniscient voice is addressing, and that this internal audience must function as an integral part of the total work. One is immediately reminded of Marlow's audience in Conrad's *Heart of Darkness*. The shipmates whom that story teller is addressing may very well symbolize the totality of the out-

---

[23] Bowra, p. 123. Thomas Greene's explanation is more "geographical". For him, the circumscribed locale of Troy required the "contrast of another plane", whereas the landscape of the *Odyssey*, obviously less confined than that of Troy, does not require so frequently the expansiveness of the epic simile (p. 55).

side world, but in the literal confines of the story they function as little more than auditors, allowing Marlow simply an occasion to tell his story of Kurtz. Except for the psychological verisimilitude of Marlow telling his story to someone, one wonders why Conrad bothered to enclose the Marlow narration within the boundaries of a larger setting and why so much time was spent introducing the reader to an internal audience whose function, if it can be defended at all, remains indefinable. The internal audience of Ulysses' narration in the *Odyssey*, however, represents more than a mechanical function. As I have pointed out in the first chapter, it is the Phaeacians listening to their *aidos* Demodocus who conveniently and convincingly set up the Ulysses story. Moreover, once they have heard him, "all [holding] their peace throughout the covered cloister, enthralled by the charm of his story", they are now completely sure that this man is the great hero they suspected him to be, and they confirm with rich gifts their offer of safe convoy back to Ithaca.

As there exists a dramatic relationship between story teller and auditor, so does there exist an equally dramatic relationship between auditor and his effect on the story teller. It is interesting to note that the parts of the *Odyssey* which have come under heaviest critical censure through the centuries have been the fabulous episodes of Ulysses' wanderings. As Ker points out, the romantic elements in the *Odyssey* were probably not believed even by the auditors in its own day, whereas "many of them must have had their grandmothers' testimony for things like the portents before the death of the suitors.[24] Considering what we know of crafty Ulysses as a story teller in less spectacular parts of the *Odyssey* and remembering that all the fabulous episodes occur during *his* narration, one would hardly be accused of idle speculation in wondering how much of Ulysses' story can be interpreted as a device by which to impress the Phaeacians rather than simply as a story for its own sake. It is true that in both of his earlier accounts of the shipwreck, the first spoken to Nausicaa and the second to King Alcinous and Queen Arete in Book VI, Ulysses tells the whole story truthfully. But this kind of truthfulness is an exception in Ulysses' other experiences. Danger has taught him to appraise the situation and tell the kind of story that would cause him the least harm or the most good. The first example of this craftiness we see in the *Iliad* where, in reporting Agamemnon's "peace" offering to the recalcitrant Achilles, Ulysses conveniently excises the part that he feels would cause Achilles to refuse – Agamemnon's

[24]   W. P. Ker, *Epic and Romance*, p. 15.

insistence on his rights of seniority and royalty.[25] We see again in the *Odyssey* how in each of his encounters with the people on Ithaca – Minerva in disguise, Eumaeus, Antinous, Penelope and Laertes – Ulysses rejoices not only in confirming his disguise with an appropriate story but also in embellishing the story with a multitude of unnecessary details. He is "glad" when he hears Penelope in Book XVIII "trying to get presents out of the suitors, and flattering them with fair words which he knew she did not mean". He is almost sadistic in teasing Laertes about his own identity after all danger from the suitors had disappeared, fabricating a wild story about his coming from Alybas, the son of King Apheidas, to meet Ulysses and exchange presents.[26]

Would it be too ingenious to suggest that the fabulous elements in Ulysses' narrative are fabulous only because Ulysses is narrating them? Certainly it is clear from the introductory lines that modulate into his large narration that Ulysses is crafty enough to tell the Phaeacians stories they *want* to hear. The account of his voyages, after all, is related not only in answer to Alcinous's question: "Where have you been wandering?" but also in answer to his command: "Tell us of the people themselves, and of their cities – *who were hostile, savage, and uncivilized and who, on the other hand hospitable and humane.*" [27] Alcinous earlier had pointed with understandable pride to the hospitality of the Phaeacians, to their advanced civilization (now almost become soft), and to their charitable habit of escorting ship-wrecked foreigners back to their homes. His question, then, seems as much a subtle invitation for Ulysses' praise by contrasting his people with the barbarousness of other civilizations as it is an open invitation for Ulysses to tell of his wanderings. And Ulysses, sensitive always to the demands of his safety and his total dependence on the good will of his guests, complies.

Of the ten different episodes he narrates, Ulysses in effect categorizes various kinds of *in*hospitality, in direct and almost unsubtle contrast to the treatment he is at the moment receiving. Of violent, barbarous inhospitality, he cites two examples: the Cyclops and the Laestrygonians. And those details about the Cyclops that he stresses are arranged in diametric opposition to the attributes of the Phaeacians that Alcinous had earlier boasted of. Whereas the Phaeacians welcome with open arms all wanderers and suppliants, feasting, dressing and convoying them back home, the Cyclops devours his "guests". Whereas the

[25]   IX, 162.
[26]   XXIV, 302 ff.
[27]   VIII, 572 ff.

Phaeacians enjoy the comforts of cleanliness – warm baths and frequent changes of linen – the Cyclops leaves his dung in unholy heaps all around the cave. The royal palace of the Phaeacians is surrounded by a "large garden of . . . four acres with a wall around it . . . full of beautiful trees" cultivated and irrigated; the natural habitat of the Cyclops is wild and completely uncultivated, his only palace a cave.[28] The Phaeacians are master mariners; the Cyclops can only stand on the shore and throw huge boulders at the sea-nimble Ulysses. The smaller details might be multiplied, but the effect is the same. Ulysses deliberately ingratiates himself by praising the hospitality of his guests. And his praise is not an explicit commendation of their civilization. Such a gesture would have offended against the dictum which insists that a suppliant is entitled by divine command to hospitality. Rather its oblique praise for the Phaeacians is arrived at by describing with gruesome details the suffering that results from *in*hospitality.

The Laestrygonian episode, though much shorter than the Cyclops episode, is similar in its series of contrasts. Ulysses, however, makes added use of the wicked queen whom his men discover to be "a giantess as huge as a mountain" and who calls her husband to kill the visitors. She functions clearly, of course, as foil to Queen Arete.

Of inhospitality disguised as a good, Ulysses tells the story of Circe who functions, presumably, as foil to Nausicaa. Whereas Homer takes great pains to characterize the Phaeacian princess as a maiden pure in heart and in body, a saviour of the ship-wrecked Ulysses, Circe is characterized as an erotic goddess, whose eroticism is perhaps allegorically related to her transforming of men into pigs. Mercury's offering to Ulysses of an antidote that would counteract Circe's porcine drug and his suggestion that she will indiscriminately offer any man her body if he is able to resist her magic add to the picture of her as a divine nymphomaniac. Nausicaa, on the other hand, is described as a beautiful maiden innocent of sexual impurity. Homer's almost unsubtle attempt at characterizing her purity by way of image interplay – the long description of her washing clothes scrupulously clean at the riverside followed by an epic simile comparing her beauties to those of Diana – interacts successfully with his description of her innocent refusal to run away from the half-drowned Ulysses and her prudent wish to avoid scandal by suggesting that he follow behind the waggons on their return to court. Alcinous's desire, later expressed, to keep Ulysses at Phaeacia as a

[28] "Now the Cyclops neither plant nor plough . . . and live on such wheat, barley and grapes as grow wild without any kind of tillage." IX, 105 ff.

husband for Nausicaa contributes further to characterizing her as a type of "Britomartian" chastity. Ulysses' subsequent description of the eroticism of Circe, therefore, would be recognized by the Phaeacians as a tribute to the purity of their princess.

The episode of the lotus eaters, the shortest adventure of the ten episodes, also exemplifies a type of inhospitality – that of euphoric imprisonment. Alcinous's request to Ulysses that he remain on the island as husband to Nausicaa is qualified by his explanation that "no one (heaven forbid) shall keep you here against your own wish"; whereupon he immediately arranges for Ulysses' safe convoy back to Ithaca. Again, the contrast is functional. Like the land of the lotus eaters, Phaeacia offers Ulysses every conceivable happiness: an advanced civilization, a lovely wife, a royal position, heroic fame. But the Phaeacian offer is gratuitous and unconditional. The euphoria offered not only by the lotus eaters but by Calypso and Circe as well can only be purchased at the price of freedom. For Ulysses, an uncertain and dangerous future in freedom is preferable to a euphoric present in slavery, and his dramatization of this preference in the episodes narrated to the Phaeacians pays tribute to their own gratuitousness.

Except for the episodes of the Sirens and of Scylla and Charybdis – which can be dismissed here as examples of destruction by surprise and chicanery (one destroying its victims by attraction and the other by repulsion) – the episodes remaining can be characterized not by the host's offense against hospitality but by the "indiscretions" of guests. Although Ulysses in his great narrative would have the Phaeacians see him as a suffering hero, buffeted unmercifully by the gods and by the inhumanity of other men, he recognizes at the same time that offense against hospitality is not always one-sided. Naturally in the three episodes so functioning it is the crew who commit this offense against Ulysses' orders. The first example with the Ciconians describes Ulysses' men loth to leave Ciconia after the sack, foolishly gorging themselves on wine and allowing the conquered to reorganize and drive the invaders out. The second example of the crew's folly is described in the Aeolus incident in which, after the god of the winds has feasted the Greeks for a month, he ties up the winds in a sack in order to assure Ulysses a safe voyage home. The crew, envious of what they think are gifts awarded to Ulysses alone, foolishly untie the sack and thereby unloose the winds, driving the ships far off course. The final episode of guests' offense against hosts dooms the men to Jove's anger and they perish. Against the explicit command of Ulysses, the men slaughter and eat the sacred cattle of Hyperion. Having been warned against such an act both by Circe and Tiresias, their punishment is eminently just.

The episode of Ulysses' voyage to the underworld at first glance seems to deviate from the pattern of story with which Ulysses answers Alcinous's question. But despite the fact that it reads like a short sequel to the *Iliad*, each of the famous heroic warriors of that poem making his appearance and by his or Ulysses' account bringing the reader up to date on his post-*Iliad* experiences, the center of the episode is in reality closely concerned with the pattern of answer that Ulysses had been rehearsing. In Agamemnon's lament for his fate at the hands of Aegisthus and Clytemnestra, Ulysses dramatizes the most infamous kind of inhospitality – a man murdered in his own house by one who has already cuckolded him. And in his mother's and Tiresias's account of the present situation in Ithaca, Ulysses is able to parallel the generous hospitality of his own household with what the Phaeacians are at the moment showing him – with the ironic difference that the guests at his home have offended against all canons of behavior and have violated by their excesses the sacred relationship between host and guest. The Hades episode, therefore, not only works, as did all the others, as a foil to the treatment Ulysses is at the moment enjoying, but it functions too as an introduction for Ulysses' return to Ithaca. In this respect, it bridges the first half of the epic with the second by dramatizing that what *is* at the moment in Ithaca scarcely resembles what *is* at the moment in Phaeacia, that the actual and the ideal are disturbingly, almost tragically, disparate, and that the principle of order must by violence be restored.

6

The preceding pages have offered evidence that Homer never made use of the restricted voice in the *Odyssey* as a thinly disguised mouthpiece for his own voice. The timbre of restricted voice was shown to be different from the omniscient in respect to the source of knowledge from which each of the narrations could be told, in respect to the judicious distinctions in use of epic simile, and in respect to the internal dramatic function that the audience of the delegated narration plays in the epic. But Ulysses' memorable narration of his wanderings represents only one, though obviously the longest and the most important, example of delegated narration in the *Odyssey*. There exist two others, shorter and less spectacular, but artistically very important.

The first example comes early in the epic, before the hero himself appears on the scene. Encouraged by Athena to search for his father,

Telemachus proceeds first to Pylos in order to visit Nestor. The meeting is more than friendly; Nestor feasts the visitors and answers Telemachus as fully as he can. Nestor's story, which makes up most of Book III, fulfills a number of functions which the totally omniscient voice of the *Iliad* had never attempted. In the first place, the occasion of the story is itself emotionally moving. Nestor's meeting with the son of his warrior friend is dramatically appropriate, for it brings together the old and the new Hellas, Nestor nostalgically recalling the days of former glory and Telemachus looking forward to restoring that glory in Ithaca by finding his father. The meeting also succeeds in dramatizing the cruelty of war as well as its glory by bringing together a son deprived of his father for twenty years and a father deprived forever of his son, the hero Antilochus slain at Troy.

But more important than the dramatic occasion of Nestor's story is the movement from the omniscient voice of the first two books to the restricted voice of the third. Nestor's story is really divided into three parts and serves a triple function. First, he describes the quarrel between Agamemnon and Menelaus over the time necessary to propitiate the gods with sacrifice. Half of the Greek force, including Nestor, Ulysses and Diomede, agree to sail home with Menelaus immediately; the other half agree to remain with Agamemnon and offer hecatombs. After the first group sail to Tenedos, a second quarrel ensues when Ulysses, counter to the wishes of Menelaus, Diomede and Nestor, wishes to return to Agamemnon and make peace. This is the last that Nestor ever hears of Ulysses, and as such his story begins to fill in the details prerequisite even to Ulysses' own story which does not rehearse these early events. The second part of Nestor's narration serves as a kind of short sequel to the *Iliad* (much as the Hades episode did) as he reveals the fates of some of the heroes who fought at Troy. The third part of Nestor's narrative, characteristic of both the major and minor delegated narrations, serves the function of ironic parallelism. The account of Agamemnon's murder, its importance in the epic underscored in the next book by Menelaus's more detailed version of the event, would have been interpreted by most Neo-Classical critics as mere episode. But in reality the event is closely related to the main action by paralleling ironically in microcosm the fate of the hero in the larger action. Four major characters populate Nestor's account of Agamemnon's homecoming – Agamemnon himself, Clytemnestra, Aegisthus and Orestes. Four major characters, of course, are involved in Ulysses' homecoming – the hero himself, Penelope, the suitors (considered as a unit), and

Telemachus, the fates of the latter ironically paralleling the fates of the former. Clytemnestra, the unfaithful wife, is foil to the heroically faithful Penelope; Aegisthus, the "suitor" who *slays* the returning hero, is contrasted to Penelope's suitors who *are slain* by the returning hero; Agamemnon, the slain victim, is foil to Ulysses, the slayer; and Orestes, the bloody avenger, is contrasted to Telemachus whose restraining activity among the suitors is, though less spectacular than Orestes' vengeance, at least somewhat responsible for the happy ending.

The second example of the delegated narration occurs in Book IV. Including Menelaus's answer to Telemachus's questions about his father, it extends for 261 lines, in some instances corroborating Nestor's story and in other instances adding details that Nestor could not have known. The effect of such an accumulation of detail does two things: 1) It leads up to Ulysses' own narration which then becomes the large complement of the two introductory stories, and 2) by preceding not only Ulysses' own story but his very appearance it creates a suspense about the details of Ulysses' whereabouts (though not of his general fate – the argument of Book I having told us of his imprisonment on Calypso's island).

As in Book III, the occasion of this delegated narration is significant. Telemachus, accompanied by Pisistratus, Nestor's son, is entertained royally by Menelaus and Helen who are celebrating the marriage of their daughter Hermione to Achilles' son. Menelaus's courteous remarks to Pisistratus about Nestor's good fortune in having so many good sons to accompany him into old age underscores the fact of Helen's sterility. Though never pursued, the subject would seem to suggest Homer's attitude about the punishment accorded Helen for her sin. The archetypal situation of the beautiful woman, sterile in marriage, seems subtly exploited here.[29] Further, the offhand mention of Helen's spinning as she converses with the two visitors, portraying as it does a scene of domestic order, contrasts ironically with the use of Penelope's needlework, a ruse to stave off the desperate suitors. The contrast becomes all the more ironic, of course, when the obvious fact that she who has caused the domestic chaos in Ulysses' home (not to mention the untold suffering in thousands of other Greek and Trojan homes) is portrayed as reunited with her cuckolded husband while the faithful couple, Penelope and Ulysses, are separated by hundreds of miles and two decades.

Menelaus's story itself adds important details to Nestor's brief version

[29]   Helen's only child was a daughter, Hermione. She had no further children by Menelaus.

about the eight-year journcy. In addition, it reveals some first-hand information about Agamemnon's murder which contributes further ironic parallels to the Ulysses homecoming, parallels which Nestor's story had not included. It is curious, for example, that Menelaus's version of Agamemnon's murder makes no mention of Clytemnestra's perfidy but rather concentrates largely on the details of the unfaithful watchman and the banquet ambuscade. Aside from the fact that any dwelling on Clytemnestra's role in the murder would have embarrassed Helen who was part of Menelaus' audience, it would seem that the emphasis on the watchman and ambuscade complements Nestor's version, which omits these details, and looks forward by ironic anticipation to the resolution of the poem. As Agamemnon, Clytemnestra, Aegisthus and Orestes function in Nestor's story as foils to Ulysses, Penelope, the suitors and Telemachus, so does the unfaithful watchman, who reports to Aegisthus Agamemnon's landing, function as foil to the faithful swineherd Eumaeus and the faithful old serving-maid Euryclea, who keep their master's identity a secret and participate fully in his final revenge, which ironically turns out to be a banquet ambuscade of a different kind.

III. THE *ARCADIA*

1

My decision to include the *Arcadia* in a study proposing to examine critically the major epics of the English Renaissance rests on an assumption that has not been universally accepted by the world of scholarship. The assumption, of course, is that the *New Arcadia* [1] is an epic. Perhaps this problem of generic identification has been at the center of most of the critical controversy over Sidney's work. Bertram Dobell (who as "discoverer" of the *Old Arcadia* probably had a vested interest in praising the original and disparaging the revision) could only see the *New Arcadia* as "formless and grotesque", its plot "overlaid and confused" with many independent stories "unskilfully pieced together". [2] Even sympathetic critics of the *New Arcadia*, like S. L. Wolff, who have testified to the "almost incredible skill" of Sidney in reweaving his story "upon the loom of Heliodorus", insist that "such marvellous involution and complexity defeat their own artistic ends". [3] On the other hand, those critics who have argued for the epic intention of the *New Arcadia*

---

[1] I shall appropriate the traditional distinctions and refer to Sidney's original version as the *Old Arcadia* and the revision published in 1590 as the *New Arcadia*. But my discussion of the *New Arcadia* does not extend to the composite version of 1593. I agree with Joan Rees that "we have no guarantee that the revised end of the *Old Arcadia* for which Lady Pembroke held the notes was to correspond with the end of the *New Arcadia* of which Greville was the trustee". In "Fulke Greville and the Revisions of *Arcadia*", *Review of English Studies*, XVII (Feb., 1966), 55. It may be true, as C. S. Lewis has asserted, that for the literary *historian* the *Arcadia* must mean the composite text of 1593 because it was the text that Shakespeare, Milton and Lamb knew; but for the *structural critic* any conclusions about Sidney's artistry that are based on dubious assumptions about the legitimacy of this text would be suspect.

[2] Bertram Dobell, "New Light upon Sir Philip Sidney's *Arcadia*", *Quarterly Review*, CCXI (July, 1909), 81-82.

[3] S. L. Wolff, *The Greek Romances in Elizabethan Prose Fiction* (New York, 1912), p. 352.

see artistic merit in its pages. Greenlaw,[4] Brie,[5] and Goldman [6] all point to Sidney's contemporaries as having recognized the work as epic and add their own corroborating interpretations, the first two scholars, however, exaggerating the allegorical elements. It is with Kenneth O. Myrick's full-length treatment of the problem that criticism of the *New Arcadia* as epic comes to its fruition.[7] His thesis, supported convincingly by John F. Danby,[8] E. M. W. Tillyard,[9] and C. S. Lewis,[10] is that in both theme and structure the *New Arcadia* answers to many of the requisites for epic laid down by Renaissance critics, particularly Minturno, and by Sidney himself in the *Defense of Poetry*.[11] In theme, for example, Sidney expands his almost exclusive emphasis on love and friendship in the *Old Arcadia* to include the heroic and the martial in the *New Arcadia*.[12] In setting, the events limited geographically to Arcadia itself in the original he expands to bring in all of Greece and even Asia Minor in the revision. "Love, adventure, politics, heroic warfare, and great national and even international events . . . all appear in the *New Arcadia*. Warfare and great events are absent from the *Old Arcadia*." [13]

But the chief technique of transformation from romance to epic is

---

[4]   Edwin A. Greenlaw, "Sidney's *Arcadia* as an Example of Elizabethan Allegory", *Kittredge Anniversary Papers* (1913), pp. 327-337 and "The Captivity Episode in Sidney's *Arcadia*", *Manly Anniversary Studies* (1923), pp. 54-63.
[5]   *Sidney's Arcadia* (Berlin, 1918); a German work, it is conveniently summarized in Zandvoort's *Comparison*, pp. 124-133.
[6]   Marcus S. Goldman, *Sir Philip Sidney and the Arcadia* (Urbana, Illinois, 1934), Chapter VI.
[7]   Kenneth O. Myrick, *Sir Philip Sidney as a Literary Craftsman* (Cambridge, Mass., 1935).
[8]   John F. Danby, *Poets on Fortune's Hill* (London, 1952), p. 71.
[9]   E. M. W. Tillyard, *The English Epic and its Background* (London, 1954), p. 297 ff.
[10]   C. S. Lewis, *Sixteenth Century English Literature* (Oxford, 1955), p. 335 ff.
[11]   Myrick, Chapter IV.
[12]   Even Walter R. Davis, whose recent study of the *Arcadia* insists that the work is not epic but only highly developed pastoral romance, implicitly admits the presence of much epic material. Seriousness, completeness, thematic density, ambivalence – all terms which Davis has used to characterize the changes that Sidney brought to his revision – would seem to bespeak some manner of epic intention. Moreover, by admitting that Sidney "qualified the optimism of pastoral romance in order to bring its vision closer to observed human reality" and that the work "exhibits the ambivalence rather than the innocence of the human condition", Davis seems to have exaggerated his own concern with the generic identity of the *Arcadia*. See his "A Map of Arcadia: Sidney's Romance in Its Tradition" in *Sidney's Arcadia* with Richard A. Lanham (New Haven, 1965), pp. 178-179.
[13]   Myrick, p. 129.

more noticeably structural than thematic. As in the *Odyssey*, the *Aeneid*, and the *Ethiopica* (Sidney knew the first two in the original and the latter in Underdowne's translation), the *New Arcadia* begins *in medias res* and delegates to characters the necessary expositions. It begins (if we discount the Strephon-Claius-Urania scene as a kind of dramatized invocation [14]) with the shipwreck of Musidorus and Pyrocles, the pre-requisite action later being narrated by Kalander and by the two princes themselves, along with a host of subordinate narrators. In the *Old Arcadia*, of course, Sidney had begun omnisciently *ab ovo* with the details of Basilius's retreat and the circumstances of Musidorus and Pyrocles coming to Arcadia. The narrative complications necessarily resulting from this *in medias res* revision of an already involved *ab ovo* plot must have been staggering for Sidney; and his very decision to proceed with the revision is impressive evidence of his desire to invest his earlier "idle work" with epic dignity. That he himself probably considered the results of the revision to be "heroicall" is clear from his laudatory description in the *Defense of Poetry* of Heliodorus's *Ethiopica*, an *in medias res* work Sidney largely modeled his revision after, particularly in the opening shipwreck scene.[15] Nor would Sidney have been bothered by whatever hybridization resulted from revising pastoral into epic. "Some have mingled matters Heroicall and Pastorall", he wrote in the *Defense*, "but that commeth all to one in this question, for if severed they be good, the conjunction cannot be hurtfull." [16]

With this assumption stated, the proper business of this chapter – a critical examination of Sidney's narrative artistry in the *New Arcadia* – can begin. My inclusion of his work here, though determined in part by the testimony of eminent scholars who have judged it to be epic, is chiefly motivated, as the rest of the chapter will attempt to demonstrate, by my judgment that Sidney's use of the *in medias res* structure testifies to a narrative artistry that is more complex and sophisticated than has hitherto been established.

2

Few studies have considered the architectonics of the *New Arcadia* worthy of their attention. Too often, critics have been content to dismiss

---

[14] Myrick, p. 115 ff.; but see Davis, *Sidney's Arcadia*, p. 84 ff. for a symbolic reading.
[15] Albert Feuillerat, ed., *The Prose Works of Sir Philip Sidney* (Cambridge, 1962 reprinting), vol. 3, p. 10. All subsequent references to Sidney's works will be to this edition of four volumes.
[16] P. 22.

its complex structure with epithets that fail to approximate Sidney's plan. "A return to the older form of chivalric fiction" [17] – "the Spanish fashion of dovetailing many side-stories into the main plot" [18] – "rewoven upon the loom of Heliodorus" [19] – "interlocked and endlessly varied narrative" [20] – all these phrases attest to a certain weakness of critical insight into the structure of the *New Arcadia*. Even the more sympathetic critics have generally avoided a close study of its architectonics. Zandvoort, in his famous work,[21] moves away from the Dobellians, who see little merit in Sidney's revision, and cautiously prefers it over the *Old Arcadia*, but this book is more a compendium of textual, bibliographical and comparative problems than it is a critical study. Myrick devotes two full chapters to the fable-episode distinction and seems more inclined than any of his predecessors to unravel the intricate weave of Sidney's art, but even in this book the criticism serves as an example for a separate thesis, which, as I have already pointed out, is concerned with the problem of generic identification: that is, the *New Arcadia* is an epic, among other reasons, because Sidney made use of epic episodes. In more recent studies, John F. Danby conducts a brilliant examination of Sidney's characterization, but except for a few incisive thrusts into its plot,[22] he shows no interest in identifying a structural pattern. Frederick S. Boas's critical biography [23] merely synopsizes the two versions, his work thus becoming a handy aid to memory for scholars but less than valuable as a piece of criticism. Walter R. Davis,[24] on the other hand, has offered significant insights into the theme of Sidney's work and has written probably the best long study on the subject. His strategy in accepting the 1593 composite version as "canonical", however, forces him into questionable final judgments about Sidney's "pastoral" intention and to scant the epic structure of the work.

An imposing of the "epic voice" criticism (which has been outlined in theory in Chapter I and applied to the *Odyssey* in Chapter II) on the *New Arcadia* will offer at least a tentative solution to the problem of

---

[17] Dobell, 89.
[18] Mario Praz, "Sidney's Original *Arcadia*", *London Mercury*, XV (March, 1927), 509.
[19] Wolff, p. 352. Wolff's study of structure in the *New Arcadia* pays little or no heed to narrator and audience despite his detailed summary of the plot.
[20] Lewis, *Sixteenth Century English Literature*, p. 334.
[21] *Sidney's Arcadia: A Comparison Between the Two Versions* (Amsterdam, 1929).
[22] *Poets on Fortune's Hill* (London, 1952), pp. 76-78.
[23] *Sir Philip Sidney* (London, 1955).
[24] See n. 12.

Sidney's structural design. Certainly the large distinction between the omniscient voice and the delegated voice or voices is perfectly applicable to the *New Arcadia*. Moreover, if the reader looks at the work not as a bewildering jumble of characters and episodes but rather as a narrative whose "fable" is augmented and enriched by the various narrations of a few characters in the main plot, the superficial bewilderment clears up. Viewed panoramically, the relationship between omniscient and delegated narration in the *New Arcadia* is no more complex than that of the *Odyssey*. In the latter poem, the major delegated narration occurs roughly in the middle (Books IX through XII), the minor delegated narrations occur near the beginning (Nestor's and Menelaus's stories in Books III and IV), and the uninterrupted omniscent narration (from the return of Ulysses to the slaying of the suitors) takes place at the end, Books XIII to XXIV. The *New Arcadia*, for all its multiplication of characters and episodes, follows the same large pattern. Because there are two heroes, Sidney allows each to narrate a considerable bulk of the story in Book II. The minor delegated narrations, though scattered throughout the first two books, are concentrated in Book I. And the uninterrupted omniscient narration comprises all that is left of Book III.

Viewed from within, of course, the *New Arcadia* presents more intricate problems. And yet it is possible to reduce the network of episodes that bisect and trisect each other to a maximum of eight narrators, five of whom are central characters in the main action – Musidorus, Pyrocles, Pamela, Philoclea and Basilius – and only three who can be considered minor – Kalander, his steward and Helen of Corinth. These eight narrators tell thirteen stories, four of which present no complex problem because they narrate exposition closely related temporally to the main action which the omniscient narrator could easily have narrated himself. Three of the narrations, though the longest, are simply exposition of the pre- *in medias res* action, Musidorus's and Pyrocles' account of their life and adventures up to the time of the shipwreck and Kalander's account of the royal family. By this count, six narrations are left. Although they tend to complicate the plot more than the other eight, the characters they introduce return to the main action of Book III. Perhaps a disinction among the four kinds of narration that Sidney delegates to his characters will be useful here.

(1) *Primary delegated narrations.* – These narrations are akin to Ulysses' in the *Odyssey*. They are both primary and necessary – primary because they are concerned with the heroes, are narrated by them and comprise much of Book II (Chapters 6-10 and 18-24); necessary be-

cause Sidney chose to begin his work omnisciently with the shipwreck scene *in medias res* and was forced to return to the pre- *in medias res* action by way of restricted narrators. A third narration I would include under this heading: Kalander's account of the royal family, the Delphian oracle and Basilius's rustic retreat (Book I, Chapters 3 and 4). It is of primary importance because it not only introduces the heroines who are finally to be paired off with the two princes but because it introduces the political conflict as well. Like the Musidorus-Pyrocles narration, it is necessary because it is related directly to the main action and in a past time. In the *Old Arcadia*, Sidney had narrated the Basilius story in the omniscient voice and the princes' backgrounds in the eclogues.

(2) *Secondary delegated narrations.* – These narrations are secondary because their reach into past time does not extend to events before the *in medias res* beginning. That is to say, when for reasons of plot advancement Sidney separates the heroes, he usually narrates omnisciently the progress of only one, allowing the other to re-create the "passed over" events in his own words. It is, in other words, exposition of action *since* the *in medias res* beginning. From the aspect of good narrative, these stories represent Sidney's least successful effort. Not forced to delegate these narrations as he was the pre- *in medias res* action, Sidney could with equal convincingness have moved his omniscient focus to the other character with a simple "meanwhile". It is true, of course, that suspense and restricted characterization are served by this device; but unfortunately, because there are three such narrations – Zelmane-Pyrocles to Musidorus (Book I, Chapters 13 and 14), Dorus-Musidorus to Zelmane-Pyrocles (pp. 153-158), and Pamela to Philoclea (pp. 178-182) – their presence tends to complicate the other narrations which would have stood out in bolder relief without this unnecessary competition.

(3) *Tangential delegated narrations.* – These are the least classical kind of episode because they seem to complicate the main action unnecessarily. One wonders, however, whether the complication is caused more by jaded twentieth-century memories than by any defect in Sidney's art. Although they introduce a host of characters that seem only tangentially related to the main plot, we discover in Book III that the tangents move centripetally by returning each of the characters to the main action in a significant way. Moreover, for all their complication, there are only three such narrations – all of which come in Book I: Kalander's steward's story of Argalus and Parthenia (pp. 31-37), Helen of Corinth's story of Amphialus and herself (Book I, Chapter 11), and Basilius's story of Phalantus and Artesia (pp. 97-100).

(4) *Exposition to the primary delegated narration.* – Although all delegated narrations serve the obvious function of exposition, there are three stories – concerned with the Erona, Plangus, Antiphilus triangle – which really can be considered exposition to the exposition. Musidorus's and Pyrocles' account of their role in the Queen Erona siege leaves the exposition to that episode unexplored. Because the chief characters in this scene would very likely have become the instruments of Euarchus's return to the main action of Book III had Sidney finished his revision, it was incumbent upon him to keep the details of this scene constantly in the reader's attention. This he does by telling the story in three installments and from the mouths of narrators other than the princes, who obviously could not have been privy to all the facts. By hearing the account in staggered (though complementary) versions and at interrupted times from the mouths of Philoclea (Book II, Chapter 13), Pamela (Book II, Chapter 15), and Basilius (Book II, Chapter 29), Pyrocles as sole audience to the narrations and as son of Euarchus would certainly have figured in his father's epic return to the main action.

3

The first serious point of view difficulty which confronts the critic is the double problem of 1) dramatic modulation from omniscience to restriction, and 2) the functionalism of the *recitation* of the episode itself once that modulation has taken place. As we observed in the *Odyssey*, the progression from omniscient narration to restricted narration (made necessary, of course, by the author's commitment to an *in medias res* structure) requires a reasonable motive. Any peremptory, unprepared transference from the autonomy of omniscience to the dependence of restriction would fail to convince the reader that the omniscient narrator has indeed "given up" his authority and delegated it to one of his characters. Furthermore, once he has committed his narrative to a new voice, it is incumbent upon him to connect the recitation of the restricted narration to the main action in some significant way. Or, by way of a metaphor from music, the foreign key must be both prepared for in the committed or home key and must itself act harmonically to carry forward the design of the home key once the return is made. We have already commented on Homer's remarkable success in using the Phaeacian banquet and the bard, Demodocus, as a dramatic occasion for Ulysses' narration, and in using the recitation itself as an immediate cause of his convoy back to Ithaca. Are the delegated narrations equally well prepared for in the *New Arcadia*? Is there a reasonable motive for the modulation from the omniscient voice; and is the main action moved forward by the recitation of the narrative itself?

There is no question that the primary delegated narrations answer to these problems very well. Musidorus's narration is prepared for by his slow but subtle penetration of Basilius's retreat in his disguise as the shepherd Dorus and by his strategy in awakening Pamela to his true identity by feigning love to her attendant, Mopsa. In essence, the entire narration is a kind of love song to Pamela as well as a slow dramatic confirmation of Musidorus's heroic identity to one who had suspected it.[25] By its *de facto* recitation, Musidorus's narration also serves to forward the plot. Unlike the *Aeneid*, where the love affair between Aeneas and Dido is preliminary to the main action, Aeneas's narration thus stirring the affections of a character who does not ultimately participate in the resolution, the love of Musidorus and Pamela in the *New Arcadia* would have served as a central incident in the resolution.[26] And thus Musidorus's narration succeeds in occasioning the initial rapport between the lovers. Indeed, it serves a very important mechanical device as well. Anxious in his suit as a result of Pamela's acceptance of his story, Musidorus chances a kiss and is severely reprimanded. Because of his temporary banishment from her favor, Musidorus is absent from the company when it is abducted by Cecropia's forces, a convenient detail that makes possible the Virgilian combat between Musidorus and Amphialus later in Book III.

Pyrocles' narration is also successful in effecting a rapport between the lovers, although its preparation seems less convincing than Musidorus's. Basilius, having made importunate advances to the embarrassed Zelmane, is rebuked by "her" and pardoned on the condition that the king send his daughter Philoclea to deliver his suit. The ruse works. Unlike the deliberate Musidorus, Zelmane reveals his identity immediately, and the narration that follows is requested by the awe-struck Philoclea. Although introduced more mechanically than the Musidorus narration, its very haste seems more appropriate to the precipitous characters of Pyrocles and Pamela than a more deliberate, cautious narration like Musidorus's would have been. Indeed, the manner and the occasion of their respective narrations seem entirely in keeping with the

---

[25] In this latter sense of revelation and confirmation of heroic identity, this kind of narration has had classical precedents: Ulysses' story fully revealed his identity to the Phaeacians and Aeneas's story revealed his identity to Dido.

[26] In the *New Arcadia*, the third book breaks off long before the marriage of the princes and princesses, but in the original version, the marriage ends the story.

characters of the two princes as Sidney has developed them, a point that shall be examined more fully in the section on characterization.

If we include Kalander's story in the category of primary delegated narration, the modulation into his exposition of the royal family remains to be discussed. The proximate justification for the narration within the context of the main action, though not especially clever, is motivated successfully enough. Musidorus has been escorted to Kalander's home by Strephon and Claius after the shipwreck and Pyrocles' abduction by the pirates. While recuperating, he walks in Kalander's garden, sees the portrait of the royal family, and is struck by the exquisite beauty of Philoclea. Kalander's story follows naturally from Musidorus's curiosity about the painting. Kalander's recitation also furthers the main plot by moving the now sympathetic Musidorus to offer him assistance when news comes of Clitophon's capture by the Helots. It is this military venture, of course, that reunites Musidorus, as leader of the Arcadians, with Pyrocles, who had been appropriated from the pirates by the Helot rebels.

Sidney's unqualified success in modulating from one voice to another and in furthering the main plot by means of the recitation of the restricted narration is, unfortunately, limited to the primary delegated narrations. In the secondary and tangential narrations, these devices are much more erratically handled. I have already indicated that the appropriateness of the secondary delegated narrations is open to question. They represent expositions of those incidents that occur after the *in medias res* beginning, when Sidney in the omniscient voice follows only one of his heroes and must return to follow the exploits of the other. Although there are only three such episodes, their very presence in conjunction with the other narrations tends to overlay the work with restricted narrative which no amount of careful modulation can simplify.

Interestingly enough, however, and related to the problem of modulation, Sidney's decision to delegate this narration was probably motivated by a desire to satisfy what I called in the last chapter the "epistemology" of narration. In the latter two accounts, where the same details are narrated by two different people, Sidney seems to be experimenting with the differences between ontological and logical narrative truth, a device more fully developed, as we shall observe later, in Kalander's narration. What Sidney is saying here is that the ontological truth of an event can only be approximated by a speaker within the narrative, that the authority of the restricted voice is clearly limited. Thus, from Musidorus's account to Pyrocles we learn only that his recitation to Mopsa might have been successful in revealing himself to Pamela. But from Pamela's account to her sister, we learn that Pamela understands Musidorus's game, that she had suspected his true identity and that she is deeply in love with him. Whether the secondary narratives compensate "epistemologically" for their essential clumsiness of manner and occasion, however, is a moot point.[27]

Like the secondary narrations, the three tangential narrations also suffer from insufficient preparation. Yet unlike his unnecessary use of the secondary narration, Sidney's need to extend the details of the heroic siege in Book III depended on his ability to introduce enough tangential episodic complication in Book I. The least successfully motivated of the three seems to be Helen of Corinth's story. Attacked by a troop of knights after he had found Amphialus's armor and put it on, Musidorus is approached by Helen of Corinth; and mistaking him for Amphialus, she begs his forgiveness for her indirect part in Philoxenus's slaying. Musidorus reveals his identity; she asks him for safe convoy to the next town, and he agrees on the condition that "you tell me the storie of your fortune herein, lest thereafter when the image of so excellent a Ladie in so straunge a plight come before mine eyes, I condemne my selfe of want of consideration in not having demaunded thus much" (p. 66). The function of the story is not being criticized here. That problem will be reserved for later. The modulation into the restricted narration, however, as is clear from the summary, is handled only by a pretense at motivation.

Hardly more successful in this way is Kalander's steward's story of Argalus and Parthenia. When news comes of Clitophon's capture by the Helots, Kalander is understandably silenced in grief for his son's fate; and it is only natural that the steward should answer Musidorus's polite curiosity. But the length and detail of the Argalus-Parthenia episode, which is only remotely related to the immediate problem of Clitophon's imprisonment, seems artificially handled. And Sidney probably sensed the artifice when he has the steward conclude his narration with the apology: "I have all I understande touching the losse of my Lords sonne,

---

[27] Like the secondary narrations, the tangential narrations also reveal Sidney's epistemological concern for the limited authority of the restricted voice. Both Basilius and Helen of Corinth in their recitations remind their respective auditors that they have a source for their knowledge. And indeed at no point does the subject matter of their narrative transcend their knowledge of the events. Basilius's story of Phalantus, he explains to Zelmane, is made possible because one very "inward" with the knight had occasion to report it to him (p. 91). Helen knows of the details of Philoxenus's and his father's deaths and Amphialus's shame not because she is a mere mouthpiece of the omniscient voice but because "she sent a footman ... (whose faithfulness to me I well knew) from place to place to follow him, and bring me word of his proceedings." (P. 70.)

& the cause thereof: which, though it was not necessarie to Clitophons case, to be so particularly told, yet the strangenes of it, made me think it would not be unpleasant unto you". (p. 37)

The occasion of Basilius's story to Zelmane about Phalantus and Artesia is akin to the steward's about Argalus and Parthenia, a natural satisfying of curiosity on the part of the auditor – in this case Zelmane. Yet here Sidney introduces a further element which makes this tangential narration the most smoothly prepared of the three. Basilius, at this time, is lusting after Zelmane, partly because of "her" beauty, partly because he thinks she will participate significantly in future events predicted by the oracle. The effect of the story, narrated in a confident tone that is appropriate for a royal lover, is to anticipate with comic irony the narrative effects of the princes' stories, which serve to rouse their auditors into love for the speaker. The fact that Basilius is forced, by the exigencies of the moment, to tell the story of a lover who is being "used" by his beloved is ironically related to the final narrative disposition of his own sexual adventures with Zelmane.

No more successful than the occasions of the tangential narrations are those of the exposition to the primary delegated narration. Their staggered positions in Book II – Philoclea's and Pamela's stories serving as a kind of interlude between the major narrations of Musidorus and Pyrocles and Basilius's story as a kind of epilogue to their narrations – are not being criticized here. I have already suggested that a delegating of the whole story into three installments from the different points of view of three narrators works well. But the stilted and unnecessarily involved modulations, particularly of the first narration, leave much to be desired. The conversational exchange between Plangus and Basilius which Basilius had turned into bad verse, the theft of the verses from the bathing princesses by Amphialus's dog, Zelmane's battle with Amphialus over possession of the verses, and Zelmane's insistent curiosity about Erona's tragedy as suggested in the verses seem disproportionate in length even to the structural importance of the Plangus-Erona episode.

In summary, one might safely say that Sidney's attitudes towards artistic modulation from omniscient to restricted narration seem to have been determined by the importance of the restricted narration. He demonstrates a remarkable skill in introducing the three major delegated narrations; but he is often careless in modulating to minor narrations, sometimes being abruptly mechanical, sometimes annoyingly periphrastic, only occasionally convincing. More evident is his skill in making the narration itself further the main action. The matching of the lovers is clearly effected by the narrations of Musidorus and Pyrocles, especially the former. And the centripetal direction of the minor narration back to the main action (as shall be discussed in detail in the next section) attests to a skill in plot construction which, though perhaps too well-made for twentieth-century tastes, is commendable nonetheless.

4

One of the principal critical points made in this study is that *episode*, in its intimate relationship to the restricted point of view, functions more than adventitiously. We have already seen in the preceding section that the recitation of he episodes themselves significantly affects the movement of the main plot. And we saw in the last chapter that the classical epic related episode to the main plot by way of ironic parallelism.[28] Peculiar to the romantic epic, however, is its use of episode to introduce characters and complications whose destinies are resolved later in the *main* plot. Whereas the episodes of classical epic resolve themselves from within,[29] Sidney seldom allows his "episode" players to strut on the Arcadian stage to be heard no more. As Wolff has indicated: "he has not dropped a single thread in the whole enormous design. As far as he recast it, the grandiose pattern is perfect".[30]

Some characters who are introduced in episodes "return" to the main action as significant actors in the *New Arcadia;* others in less spectacular, though still important roles; and a few, because of the uncompleted version, may return only "conjecturally", their final disposition hinted at by the way Sidney resolved the *Old Arcadia.* Of the characters introduced in the three tangential narrations, the most important is Amphialus, the son of Cecropia. He is brought into the epic in Helen of Corinth's story in Book I of her triangular relationship with him and Philoxenus, but we do not see him as a living character until the bathing scene near the end of Book II and as the principal rebel in the siege scene that dominates Book III. Helen herself returns to the action in Book III to transport the almost dead Amphialus to Corinth. Whether she will bury or marry him we will never know.[31] The lovers introduced

---

[28] See section six of this chapter for Sidney's use of ironic parallelism or foil.

[29] None of the episode characters – Polyphemus, Circe and company – return to take part in the resolution of the *Odyssey.*

[30] Wolff, p. 353.

[31] Tillyard has pointed to Fulke Greville's mention of Amphialus's "marriage with Helena; their successions", and conjectures that Sidney must have told Greville of his further intentions. (Tillyard, p. 314 n.) I would prefer believing that Amphialus, like Hector and Turnus, noble enemies, should have died an heroic

by the steward's tangential narration in Book I – Argalus and Parthenia – are both slain by Amphialus in the siege. Phalantus, whose jousting marathon for Artesia had been narrated by Basilius in Book I, returns in Book III to do battle with Amphialus, as does Artesia herself, who conspires with Clinias to overthrow Cecropia's rebel forces and is beheaded in the Philoclea exchange. Thus, the three pairs of lovers whose stories make up the bulk of tangential narration in Book I return to make significant (in Amphialus's case, major) contributions to the resolution in Book III.

The characters from the primary delegated narration and its expository episodes present a greater problem. Anaxius, Pyrocles' nemesis, returns to help Amphialus and is finally slain by Pyrocles; but how Euarchus, king of Macedon, father of Musidorus and uncle of Pyrocles, would have returned to the story can only be conjectured. By knowing his role in the *Old Arcadia* and by examining Sidney's preparation for his return in the revision, one can assume that Euarchus would have returned to the scene by the instrumentality of Plangus. In the *Old Arcadia*, Euarchus fills the power vacuum left by the supposed death of Basilius and establishes a protectorate for Arcadia. But Sidney's revision allowed for no such device. Cecropia's rebellion had been crushed. The only heroic survivor, Anaxius, is on the verge of being slain by Pyrocles when the book breaks off. With the freeing of the prisoners imminent (the supplement supplied by Sir William Alexander actually reports it), Euarchus's original role of judge condemning his own son and nephew could not easily have been repeated. Among other reasons, of course, is that the prisoners in the *Old Arcadia* were held in captivity not by Cecropia's rebels (who had not been created then) but by Basilius's lieutenant, Philanax, who thought them responsible for Basilius's death. That Euarchus had been prepared for some kind of return, however, seems obvious by Basilius's description of Plangus's mission at the end of Book II. Erona, ready for death at Artaxia's hands, is granted a stay of execution on the condition that Plangus return with Musidorus and Pyrocles (who Artaxia mistakenly believed had been slain at sea by Plexirtus) to challenge two knights of her own choosing. Plangus, informed of the deaths of the princes, decides to seek help from Euarchus. This is the last we hear of him, of course, before the fragment breaks off. But Erona's imprisonment, Plangus's love for Erona, and the ultimate

---

death and not be resurrected, romance-like, at the end. Certainly Sidney has no compunctions about killing off both Argalus and Parthenia.

return of Euarchus seem clearly connected. How Sidney would have spliced these characters to the main action remains a problem.

Subordinate characters in the primary delegated narrations would also have figured in the resolution. The freeing of Erona would not have been effected without Artaxia, her captor, and Plexirtus, Artaxia's Cornwall-like husband, being involved. Those characters who died in the episodes – Dido, Chremes, Antiphilus, Tiridates, Andromana and the original Zelmane – would, of course, have presented no problem to Sidney. Nor would those characters whose fate had been definitely resolved at that time: Leonatus, Plangus's father, and the kings of Phrygia and Pontus. Thus, the "incredible skill" that Wolff claimed for Sidney would seem in no way indicted by the fragmentary nature of Book III. The yarn had been spun, the warp threaded, much of the woof woven. Only death's inexorable shears prevented completion.

5

The preceding analysis has shown that Sidney's concept of *episode,* though often experimental and not always successful, was more functional than "adventitious". And yet the discussion has not answered some of the larger questions rehearsed in the second chapter. In effect, it has been determined only that Sidney's sense of dramatic modulation from omniscient to restricted voice was adequate, that his use of episodic narration *per se* served plot advancement as well as simple exposition, and that the episodes which at their introduction seemed tangential actually returned their characters to the main action in a significant way. How does Sidney's complex system of episodes serve to advance characterization as well as plot? To what extent does Sidney use episode as a microcosm of the fable; or, in the language of the last chapter, do the episodes serve as parallel, ironic, or symbolic foils to the characters and incidents of the main plot?

Of the many critics who have written about the people of the *Arcadia,* none has tried systematically to analyze character by reference to the restricted narration therein. Eight characters reveal themselves and others by the stories they tell. In some instances, it is the *subject matter* of the narration itself that lends a new insight into the speaker's character; in other cases, it is the subtle difference between what the speaker *says* and what actually *is* that reveals his inner being. In any case, it is clear that Sidney's use of the restricted voice recognizes an individual behind the voice, not merely a disembodied mouthpiece for the author himself, and that the new voice succeeds in non-omniscient characterization.

It has already been suggested that Sidney makes significant distinctions in the *manner* that Musidorus and Pyrocles narrate their stories. Whereas Musidorus uses the occasion of the narrative to reveal his identity to Pamela, his narrative thus becoming a kind of prelude to their love, Pyrocles precipitously reveals his identity to Philoclea before he narrates his story, his narrative thus serving as a *coda* to their love. Equally significant, however, is the *subject matter* of their respective narrations, themes which tend to underscore the essential differences in their characters. In one of the best modern appreciations of the *Arcadia*, John F. Danby has suggested that Pyrocles' transvestite disguise can be interpreted as a touch of Sidneyan allegory stressing the synthesis of masculine and feminine in his character.[32] It is significant that the narrations which Sidney delegates to his heroes corroborate in subject matter and tone this distinction in their characters.[33] Musidorus's story contains four accounts of heroic adventure: Euarchus's wars and the princes' heroism in Phrygia, Pontus, and Galatia. In each of the accounts, right government is established after necessary military action is undertaken against tyrannies. The princes reveal themselves to be not only heroic in warfare, but also prudent and wise in political science. Significantly, from Musidorus's account of the first shipwreck and the

[32] "Pyrocles, 'a Mars's heart in a Cupid's body, the uttermost that in mankind might be seen', asserts the feminine also. His dress adds to rather than diminishes his merely masculine virtue. Throughout the story it is Sidney's intention to make Pyrocles the dominant figure. His women, though they might sometimes wear armor never do so in fact with the success of Spenser's Belphoebe. In Pyrocles, however, he would seem to be insisting that man is capable of a synthesis of qualities that includes the womanly yet avoids the hermaphroditic. The merely masculine prowess Musidorus argues for is a lesser thing than this." (P. 56.)

But for a conflicting view – that "Pyrocles' womanish dress is the mark of that spiritual effeminacy which has resulted from his allowing his reason to be ruled by passion" – see Mark Rose, "Sidney's Womanish Man", *Review of English Studies*, XV (Nov., 1964), 353-363.

[33] We recognize these differences in character early in the story. Pyrocles is first to be smitten with love for Philoclea, an immediate, all-consuming love that is effected by her portrait alone. Musidorus's love for Pamela, on the other hand, though seemingly as violent, comes only after he has found Zelmane in Basilius's retreat and views the princess, though from afar, in person. It is Pyrocles, too, who would daringly pursue his adventures without Musidorus as partner. After having defeated Tiridates, Pyrocles is challenged by a nephew of Euardes, whom the princes had slain in the siege. By his own admission, Pyrocles sets off to answer the challenge "alone ... desirous to do something without the company of the incomparable ... Musidorus, because in my hart I acknowledge that I owed more to his presence, then to anything in my self." (P. 263.)

It is Musidorus's cautiousness in following Pyrocles from a distance and coming to his assistance when Artaxia's forces would have overpowered him that saves Pyrocles' life.

princes' capture by the Phrygians to their restoring of Leonatus to the Galatian throne, not a single female character appears. Musidorus's story, then, tends to dramatize "merely masculine prowess". Pyrocles' narration, to be sure, continues the heroic adventures, but almost immediately the amatory impinges on the martial and political. Female characters suddenly crowd the scene and insinuate themselves deeply into the princes' fortunes. Dido's revenge on Pamphilus, Queen Andromana's erotic attachment to the princes, Palladius's love for the original Zelmane, Zelmane's infatuation for Pyrocles and her disguise as a page in his company – all these amatory episodes are included in Pyrocles' account of the princes' adventures and succeed – by the very fact that it is Pyrocles and not Musidorus who has chosen to narrate this part of their story – in portraying "a Mars's heart in a Cupid's body".

Kalander's narration in Book I represents a special problem of characterization. It is the best example in the *New Arcadia* of Sidney's success in characterizing the narrator himself while that same narrator is successfully engaged in characterizing others. Why Sidney devoted so much time to Kalander, clearly not a character of major importance, is not certain, except that in the process of revising his original version Kalander's story was Sidney's first attempt at delegated narration [34] and probably received the most attention. Be that as it may, the reader discovers in the old man a strategic reticence in his discussion of the royal family that, paradoxically coupled with an ordinarily characteristic verbosity, reveals him to be a kind of Sidneyan Nestor. Although he praises Basilius in the manner of the Renaissance courtier, Kalander casts serious doubt on his king's wisdom by subtly qualifying his honorifics with left-handed compliments like: "though he exceed not in the vertues which get admiration, as depth of wisdome, height of courage and largenesse of magnificence, yet is hee notable in those whiche stirre affection, as trueth of worde, meeknesse, courtesie, mercifulnesse, and liberalitie". (p. 19)

The passage from which this quotation is taken represents, significantly enough, an addition to the omniscient author's own exposition of the royal family in the *Old Arcadia*; it is a revision which pays clear tribute

---

[34] That Sidney must have been aware of Homer's strategy in delegating his voice to Ulysses in the *Odyssey* is suggested by Kalander's reference to Homer at the end of his narration. Apologizing for his verbosity, Kalander contrasts his own hospitality to Homer's, "who never entertayned eyther guestes or hostes with long speaches, till the mouth of hunger be throughly stopped" (p. 29), an almost overt reference to the Phaeacian banquet preceding Ulysses' story.

to Sidney's powers of restricted characterization and demonstrates that
the revision entailed more art than merely assigning old passages to new
speakers. For Kalander's words indicate that Sidney was acutely aware
of the differences between omniscient and restricted narration. In
Basilius's case, for example, Kalander's words might be described as
being *both* ontologically and logically true. Certainly, Basilius's "depth
of wisdom" is conspicuously absent in his superstitious adherence to the
oracle. And although his courage is advertised when he is fighting
against tailors and butchers in the commoners' revolt, it is less than
spectacular during the siege. Humanly speaking, Kalander's words also
ring true; for Basilius is Kalander's brother-in-law, married late in life
to Kalander's sister, Gynecia (a fact we learn later). A nobleman's
attitude toward his foolish king (jeopardizing as he has the safety of his
kingdom by a rustic retreat), who happens at the same time to be his
foolish brother-in-law (having submitted a wife and beautiful daughters
to the authority of a doltish shepherd), must indeed stir feelings which
can be articulated only by left-handed compliments.

In Kalander's description of Queen Gynecia, on the other hand, we
find a realistic split between ontological and logical truth. His judgment
that she has "more princely vertue" than her husband reveals an understandable regard for a sister who happens also to be his queen. But his
description of her "vehement spirits" understates a quality of energy in
Gynecia that is surpassed only by Cecropia's; and his reference to her
"unspotted chastity" takes on a sardonically ironic character when we
come to her vehemently erotic attraction for Zelmane (Pyrocles) later
in the book, an attraction made all the more ironic when it is in competition with her husband's and her daughter's.

In Kalander's description of the princesses, Pamela is characterized, as
Danby has demonstrated, as "conscious and deliberately maintained
virtue", whereas Philoclea is drawn as a "perfection of nature in which
instinctive rightness of constitution effects the same as a properly directed will. Pamela would not depart from virtue, Philoclea could not." [35]
But Danby forgets that Sidney has delegated this insight to Kalander, the
princesses' affectionate uncle and hardly a disinterested observer. Despite the near perfection of the princesses (and the princes, for that
matter), it would have been narrative folly for Sidney to have drawn
them "beatifically". If, as it has often been explained, the *Arcadia* was
written with the intention of dramatizing the moral education of a

[35]   Danby, p. 59.

gentleman or lady, then it behooved Sidney to dramatize progress, rather than eulogize perfection. That Pamela ultimately arrives at a fulfillment of "consciously and deliberately maintained virtue" cannot be denied after we follow her through the imprisonment. But the reader cannot but wonder whether her virtue earlier in the story is not at times *too* deliberate. Unlike Philoclea, who agrees immediately to marry Pyrocles when Zelmane divulges "her" identity, Pamela's withholding of assent for Musidorus after she recognizes him under the shepherd's weeds characterizes her as something of a tease. And her shocked re-action to his momentary lapse when he innocently offers to kiss her suggests that she is also something of a prude. It is her imprisonment and its attendant horrors – physical torture, atheistic confrontation in Cecropia, the supposed death of her sister – that atone for the "flaw" in her character. But in the third chapter of Book I, this kind of perfection, despite Kalander's definition of it, had not yet been realized.

If Philoclea inherits any feminine flaw in the Sidneyan creation, it is the opposite of her sister's, but even in her case, Kalander's fond eyes are blind to her imperfections. Whereas Pamela's virtue, until purified by her imprisonment, was too deliberate and cautious, Philoclea's was too spontaneous, too unrestrained by reason or decorum. Her pre-cipitousness is dramatized in a number of ways. Her almost unnatural attraction to the transvestite Zelmane before she knows the amazon's identity is only a little less decorous than her reaction when she discovers it. Overcome with joy at Pyrocles' identity, she trembles with desire and is forced to apologize for her "behaviour ill governed" and her "virgin-minde . . . stained". Love has so conquered her that she can only plead to Pyrocles: "Thou hast then the victorie: use it with vertue" (p. 260). Unlike Pamela who castigates Musidorus for one kiss innocently delivered, Philoclea, stirred by Pyrocles' narration, allows herself to be kissed repeatedly and can only remonstrate in mock anger: "Howe will you have your discourse . . . without you let my lips alone?". (p. 308) Clearly, this manner of behavior is not yet virtue "in which instinctive rightness of constitution effects the same as a properly directed will". Kalander's characterization may look forward to a "perfection of na-ture", but in Philoclea's case, as well as Pamela's, imperfection must first be purified in the crucible of suffering.

In sum, Kalander's estimate of the royal family reveals an interesting split between attitudes that are ontologically accurate and attitudes that understate or miss the mark. In Basilius's case, Kalander's reservations about his brother-in-law, though hidden in the honorifics, implicitly define the king's character. In Gynecia's case, the truth of Kalander's account is ironically reversed in the subsequent action. In the princesses' cases, Kalander defines a perfection which is less actual than potential, a perfection which only heroic suffering can later bring to fulfillment. In short, Sidney is experimenting with an unreliable narrator.

Interestingly enough, the essential distinction in the princesses' characters, which Kalander sees only in its perfectibility, becomes more accurately revealed in the very subject matter of their own narrations. Whereas Philoclea's natural warmth and optimistic exuberance tend toward the theme of love triumphant, Pamela's caution and pessimistic deliberateness tend toward the theme of love reversed. Philoclea narrates only that part of the Erona story that dramatizes successful love (albeit temporarily successful love): Erona's refusal to be married to Tiridates whom she does not love; her Juliet-like attraction to Antiphilus; their morganatic marriage; his capture by Tiridates and rescue by the princes. Philoclea's reluctance at this point to continue the story may be interpreted as a mechanical device of interlude or simply of giving Pamela a turn at narration. But it is significant that Philoclea refuses to continue the story of Antiphilus's perfidy because, by her own admission, she would prefer to end happily, or at least to be allowed some breathing time before proceeding with "horrible matter". Pamela's story, on the other hand, begins with love besmirched: Plangus's illicit relationship with Andromana; her insinuating herself into Plangus's father's attention; Andromana's Potiphar's-wife strategy against Plangus; his exile. Thus, like the significant differences in the subject matter of the princes' narrations, the princesses choose to narrate those episodes which are palatable to and revelatory of their peculiar personalities. And thus Sidney's techniques of characterization are shown more oblique and sophisticated by the use of the restricted narration of the *New Arcadia* than ever they were by the direct omniscient voice in the *Old Arcadia*.

6

One of the major suggestions in the last chapter was that Ulysses' narration of the episodes represented more than an heroic romp through Mediterranean adventures; that each of the episodes dramatized a type of *in*hospitality hateful to the gods and in total contrast to the treatment he was at the moment receiving and "negotiating" for at the hands of his auditors; that each episode was ironically related to the unjust hospitality demanded by the suitors. Those episodes narrated in his own voice, therefore, play a functional, and not merely adventitious, role in the structure of the plot and dramatization of the theme. Much of the analysis, in addition, pointed to foil characters or characteristics in the episodes which contrasted to their opposites in the main action.

That Sidney must have had something of the same in mind when he wrote the *New Arcadia* is demonstrable when one recognizes that each of the episodes dramatizes a foil to the ideals of political and amatory integrity incarnated in the princes and princesses. Greenlaw recognizes that the episodes "are by no means the haphazard type of the conventional romance", but that "they fall into two well-defined groups" given an internal unity by their allegories of politics and love.[36] Myrick, with less attachment to allegory in the stricter sense, suggests that "the lessons will be contained chiefly in the 'example' ", and that like rhetorical example, it partakes of comparison.[37]

The love of Musidorus for Pamela and Pyrocles for Philoclea, which becomes the type of ideal love in the resolution of the plot, finds its foil in almost every one of the triangles narrated in the episodes. That Sidney is conscious of this particular function of the restricted voice is obvious when he has Pyrocles say to Philoclea during his story of Queen Andromana: "Which proceeding of hers I doo the more largely set before you . . . that by the *foyle* [italics mine] thereof, you may see the noblenes of my desire to you, & the warrantablenes of your favour to me." [38] But it is not only Andromana's example that sets up the "foyle". From the most serious kind of offense against ideal love – Antiphilus's infidelity to Erona – to the most venial – the original Zelmane's insensitivity to Palladius's love – Sidney builds a hierarchy of offenses which contrasts unfavorably to the ultimate perfection of the Musidorus-Pamela, Pyrocles-Philoclea unions. Some of the episodes also parallel the imperfect love of the main action: Basilius's and Gynecia's illicit attraction for Zelmane and Amphialus's politically explosive love for Philoclea. In each episode, moreover, there exists a third party who is either a seriously culpable obstacle to the realization of true love or a relatively innocent victim of imperfect love. Yet, in no situation, except possibly Argalus's, is any character completely free from guilt in the offense against love; and no character leaves the scene unpunished for his indiscretion.

Seven such examples appear in the episodes, some closer to, others

[36] *Kittredge Anniversary Papers*, p. 331.
[37] *Sir Philip Sidney as a Literary Craftsman*, p. 243.
[38] P. 279. Pyrocles says much of the same to Philoclea when describing the original Zelmane. See p. 299.

more remote from, the main action, but all serving as foils to the principal lovers since in each case at least one of the lovers is audience to the
story. Of these, the Argalus-Parthenia episode is the most difficult to fit
into this pattern, and probably the only exception, because the degree of
culpability (if any) is hardly commensurate to the tragic resolution of
their love in Book III. The other characters lend themselves to easier
generic classification. Those who are motivated to love by physical
reasons alone include Plangus, Andromana, Pamphilus and Demagoras,
all but the latter also offending against chastity. Those who have vitiated
love by using it as a pretext to gain their own ends include Artesia,
Antiphilus, Andromana, Tiridates, Demagoras and even Plexirtus in his
political marriage to Artaxia. Those who have been used by love because
of their own naiveté include Amphialus, Phalantus, Erona, Dido and
Palladius. Those who have been unfaithful to their loved ones include
Antiphilus, Andromana and the Sidneyan Don Juan – Pamphilus. In
addition to these types, we find a dramatized commentary on royal love
misdirected (and thus parallel to Basilius's and Gynecia's indiscretions):
Helen toward Amphialus, Erona toward Antiphilus, and Plangus's
father toward Andromana.

The political "example" of the episodes is more difficult to determine
than the amatory because, as previously indicated, Euarchus's final role
in the resolution of the *New Arcadia* cannot be clearly anticipated. That
he would have represented political wisdom incarnate in Sidney's final
plan is probable from the example in the *Old Arcadia* where his
virtues are contrasted to Basilius's folly. That Sidney expected the
reader to connect Euarchus's political wisdom to the princes' is suggested
by Musidorus's lengthy account of their blood relationship and their
embarking to join him in his wars. Yet, the only substantial dramatizing
of political wisdom in the *New Arcadia* is to be found in the princes'
political adventures and not Euarchus's. How he would have solved the
Erona-Plangus-Artaxia-Plexirtus problem is less clear than his necessary
involvement with them. Therefore, in the fragment that remains, the
reader must look to Pyrocles and Musidorus as ideal rulers, or at least
potentially ideal rulers, and contrast examples of tyranny in the episodes
to their practice of justice. The examples of tyranny parallel as well the
problem of Basilius's poor leadership, for the reader recognizes their evil
characteristics not only as foils to the princes' virtues but as evil qualities
peculiar to Basilius's rule.

The wicked oligarchy which Euarchus destroys when he ascends the
Macedonian throne, for example, suggests the insufferable situation in

Arcadia itself where Basilius has delegated much of his authority to Philanax and even to the doltish Dametas. Musidorus's depreciative definition of oligarchy as "men governed . . . by a fewe, and yet . . . not taught to know what those fewe be, to whom they should obey" (p. 185) and the evil effects thereof are dramatized later in the commoner's revolt and Cecropia's rebellion. In addition, the dour king of Phrygia, "wickedly sad . . . suspecting all men of evil"; the deceived king of Pontus who takes to himself evil counsel; the Gloucester-like king of Paphlagonia who, in his infidelity to the queen, fathers a bastard son who deposes him – all these types exemplify the various degrees of Basilius's political folly and sexual lust. And the princes' success in rectifying these seriously defective political situations – not to mention their success over the Helots and Cecropia in the main action – testifies to the inherent superiority of virtue and justice in their political systems.

Thus, restricted narration in the *New Arcadia* extends to the function of ironic parallelism to the same degree that it did in the *Odyssey*. Like Homer, Sidney saw fit to use the episodes as ironic microcosmic correlaries to the macrocosm of the main action and not simply as the author's digressive opportunity "to search thro' . . . Creation for incidents or adventures for the employment of his heroes".[39] Whatever successes of dramatic modulation, plot design, oblique characterization, psychological verisimilitude and thematic foil are contained in the *New Arcadia* are directly related to Sidney's exploiting of restricted narration. All these functions, which many critics have claimed as the exclusive province of modern fiction, were conceived long ago in the minds of epic writers separated from each other by continents and centuries and yet connected by a tradition of epic voice which forced their artistry into similar channels.

[39] H. T. Swedenberg, *The Theory of the Epic in England, 1650-1800* (Berkeley, 1944), p. 203.

IV. PARADISE LOST

1

Paradise Lost is an *in medias res* epic poem which, like its structural prototype, the *Odyssey*, makes use of distinct narrating voices in the incidents and episodes of the poem. The omniscient voice, modified significantly by an abundance of heroic speeches, narrates the uninterrupted time sequence from Book I to Book V, line 562, and from the end of Adam's narration at line 559 in Book VIII to the end of the poem.[1] The major restricted voice – Raphael's – narrates from line 562 in Book V to the end of Book VII, a formidable total of 1887 lines (excluding Milton's invocation at the introduction of Book VII), and the minor restricted voice – Adam's – narrates 310 lines in Book VIII.

Because of the supernatural and supranatural argument,[2] however, clear distinctions between the omniscient and restricted voices in *Paradise Lost* are less obvious than in "natural" epics. The reader, hypnotized by the high matter of the poem, tends to hear only Milton's mighty line without differentiating among the various voices operating therein. Even when he is aware of the different voices, he tends to blur the distinction between the omniscient narration of the author and what superficially reads like the omniscience of Raphael. Hence, a preliminary step unnecessary in critical examinations of the other epics becomes necessary in *Paradise Lost*: namely, a determination of Milton's attitude toward angelic knowledge. If the restricted voice proper to all *in medias res* epics turns out to be quasi-divine and omniscient in

---

[1] My intention to isolate and describe the intricacies of restricted narration does not preclude the obviously larger and controlling role played by the omniscient speaker (see p. 23 of this study). For a valuable treatment of the point of view of the omniscient narrator, see Anne Davidson Ferry, *Milton's Epic Voice: The Narrator in Paradise Lost* (Cambridge, Mass., 1963), p. 48 ff.

[2] Theologically considered, the angels are not supernatural beings because theirs is a *created* essence.

Paradise Lost because the speaker is an archangel, then we will be forced to dismiss Milton's poem as an epic observing only mechanically the distinction between omniscient and restricted narration. On the other hand, if we find that Raphael, despite his high place in the hierarchy of created essences, does *not* know all things, then Milton is not merely aping the established *in medias res* structure while insensitive to its host of narrative ramifications, but operating successfully within an unwritten narrative tradition that rewards its hierophants with innumerable artistic secrets.

Whatever "heresies" Milton may have enunciated in his dramatization of the angels – heresies related to his interpretation of them as corporeal beings (albeit of a higher corporeality) – he generally agrees with orthodox Christian thought about angelic epistemology.[3] In the main, this agreement concerns the limitation of angelic knowledge as it relates to the intuitive quality of angelic intelligence, and the inability of the angels to know all things as God knows all things. This kind of restricted knowledge is suggested in *Paradise Lost* and clearly affirmed in the *Christian Doctrine*. Commenting on Satan's deception of Uriel, who does not know that the cherub who appears to him and asks questions about the direction of earth and Eden is Satan in disguise, Milton writes:

> For neither Man nor Angel can discern
> Hypocrisy, the only evil that walks
> Invisible, except to God alone,
> By his permissive will, through Heaven and Earth:
> And oft though wisdom wake, suspicion sleeps
> At wisdom's Gate, and to simplicity
> Resigns her charge, while goodness thinks no ill
> Where no ill seems.
>
> (III, 682-689)

And in the *Christian Doctrine*, despite his suggestion of intuitive angelic knowledge, Milton explicitly affirms its limitations:

The good angels do not look into all the secret things of God, as the Papists pretend; some things indeed they know by revelation, and others by means of the excellent intelligence with which they are gifted; there is much, however, of which they are ignorant.[4]

---

[3]   See Robert H. West, *Milton and the Angels* (Athens, Ga., 1955), p. 102.
[4]   *John Milton, Complete Poems and Major Prose*, ed. Merritt Y. Hughes (New York, 1957), p. 991. All subsequent reference to Milton's work will be to this volume.
   Despite his slap at the Papists, Milton's attitude is generally consistent with the Roman Catholic. See St. Thomas Aquinas, *Summa Theologica*, First Part, Q. 12, A. 8.

Milton's theory of restricted angelic knowledge, therefore, should logically and artistically preclude the possibility of his merely giving over to Raphael the omniscience of his own voice. Like Ulysses in the *Odyssey* and the princes and princesses in the *New Arcadia,* Raphael should function, despite his angelic nature, as a narrator limited by the time-place of his particular vantage point and not as a mere mouthpiece for the omniscient voice. Whether this expectation is fulfilled depends on Milton's deliberate distinction between the omniscient voice and Raphael's.

2

The first item of contrast recognizable between the two voices is the difference between the various shifts of focus in the omniscient narration and the relative stability of focus in the restricted. In Book V, for example, before Raphael proceeds to his narration, the omniscient author describes the archangel arriving in Eden from Heaven. The peculiar shifting of registering consciousness – from Raphael's: "To obstruct his sight [no] star interpos'd, *however small he sees*"; to the birds watching him fly by: "To all the fowls *he seems*/ A Phoenix"; to the angels guarding Paradise: "Straight *knew* him all the Bands/ Of Angels under watch"; and finally to Adam himself: "Him through the spicy Forest onward come/ Adam *discern'd*" [5] – is obviously characteristic of omniscient narration, because the consciousness extends from the inside of the "knowing" being to the outside. Such a device would be totally inappropriate to restricted narration, because restriction necessarily implies a single consciousness who may report what goes on inside other consciousnesses (usually by inference) but does not itself enter into them.

Thus, although Raphael regularly shifts his speeches from the mouth of one character to another, his narration never extends into the inner workings of that character's consciousness. His narration can extend only to the reaction of others as these reactions *appeared* to him.

> So spake th' Omnipotent, and with his words
> All seem'd well pleased, all seem'd but were not all.
> (V, 616-617)

> ... though strange to us it seem'd
> At first, that Angel should with Angel war.
> (VI, 91-92)

---

[5]   V, 255-300. Italics mine.

Which to our eyes discover'd new and strange,
A triple-mounted row of Pillars laid
On wheels (for like to Pillars most they seem'd) . . .
                                        (VI, 571-573)

Another significant item of contrast between the omniscient voice and
Raphael's is the difference between the tones of their respective narrations. Whereas the omniscient voice proceeds to its matter with an almost
presumptuous certitude, made appropriate and decorous of course by
the tradition of epic invocation, Raphael begins his story with doubts
about his ability to handle such high argument. The omniscient voice
"with no middle flight intends to soar/ Above the Aonian mount"; (I,
14-15) revisits the font of Holy Light "now with bolder wing"; (III, 53)
and follows Urania's divine voice "above the Olympian Hill . . . above
the flight of Pegasean wing" (VII, 3-4) Raphael, on the other hand, can
only apologize to Adam for the near impossibility of his task:

High matter thou injoin'st me, O prime of men,
Sad task and hard, for how shall I relate
To human sense th'invisible exploits
Of warring spirits?
                                        (V, 565-569)

And his apology is no rhetorical humility demonstrated once and then
forgotten. Rather, the angel's sense of narrative weakness reveals itself
repeatedly throughout his story:

            for who, though with the tongue
Of angels, can relate, or to what things
Liken on Earth conspicuous, that may lift
Human imagination to such highth
Of Godlike Power . . .
                                        (VI, 297-300)

And again in the next book:

            to recount Almighty works
What words or tongue of Seraphean suffice,
Or heart of man suffice to comprehend? [6]
                                        (VII, 112-114)

Such a humility suggests a dramatic distinctiveness between the omniscient narrator and the character to whom he has delegated that
narration, even though that character has not long since issued forth
from the throne of God Himself.

[6]   See also VII, 75 and VII, 177-180.

Indeed, the conscious shaping of this distinctiveness in voice has been confirmed, though unintentionally, in recent criticism of Milton by a critic who has been more denigrative than appreciative.[7] Among his various criticisms of Milton's narrative artistry, John Peter has catalogued as defects the following:

(1) "Raphael has less of a talent for vivid narration than Milton himself had shown in preceding books," his story containing vestigial traces of a vigorous rhetoric, but traces only and lacking in energy they once had.[8]

(2) "Raphael's heroic similes, like the one comparing Satan to a displaced mountain (VI, 193-198), are sometimes rather extravagant." [9]

(3) "His parentheses are nearly always awkward." [10]

(4) Raphael had edited his tale so as to make it more admonitory by interpolating two lines in the angels' song that are inappropriate to the occasion.[11]

(5) The angel "relies heavily on assertive adjectives for his effects, a debilitating makeshift which the poem often uses".[12]

Curiously enough, the very characteristics of Raphael's narration that I would list as *distinctive* to his voice Peter attacks as "narrative weaknesses". Perhaps one should be thankful that he has so conveniently listed "defects" which are really subtle virtues. Of course, one would have to agree with Peter on these points unless he understood that Milton is deliberately characterizing Raphael as a narrator in his own right whose extent of knowledge is entirely different from the omniscient voice's. Has Raphael less talent for vivid narration than Milton himself? Obviously. Raphael is not the omniscient narrator transcending time and place but a character in a story who, despite his angelic intellect, does *not* know future, contingent things, who *is* ignorant of the inner consciousness of him to whom he speaks, who, in short, is not a mere archangelical mouthpiece for the author.

---

[7]   John Peter, *Critique of Paradise Lost* (London, 1960). Peter's acknowledged indebtedness to A. J. A. Waldock's *Paradise Lost and its Critics* (Gloucester, Mass., 1947) immediately characterizes the book as denigrative. One must agree with Douglas Bush that Waldock (and by extension his disciple Peter) "reads not with the effort to understand but with the eye of a not unamiable prosecuting lawyer looking for points to score against his opponents". "Recent Criticism of *Paradise Lost*", *Philological Quarterly*, XXVIII, 43.

[8]   Peter, p. 74.

[9]   P. 74.

[10]   P. 75.

[11]   P. 28. The lines appear at the end of the angels' song: "thrice happy if they know/ Thir happiness, and persevere upright." (VII, 631-632).

[12]   P. 74.

With this point clearly in mind, it soon becomes obvious that each of
Peter's criticisms fails to take into account Milton's intention in distinguishing between the two kinds of voices. He is, as it were, attaching
a "character" or peculiar style to each of the voices and maintaining this
character or style for the duration of the recital. Thus, it is an absurdity
to say that Raphael's heroic similes are extravagant, when in fact
Raphael speaks a grand total of *three* epic similes, all of which scrupulously appropriate to the voice and audience of the occasion.[13] These
three compare, of course, to the twenty-five epic similes Milton chose to
utilize in his own voice in the first two books. To say that Raphael's
similes are often extravagant is to misunderstand that their very paucity
is functional to the intention of the restricted voice. Secondly, it is
incorrect to attack a speaker for his awkward parentheses when it is in
the very nature of restricted narration to parenthesize frequently, and if
need be, awkwardly. In each of the instances of Peter's criticism,
Raphael is constrained by the exigencies of a narration in which a being
of intuitive intellect is revealing truths to a being of discursive intellect
to backtrack briefly in order to clarify an assumption which Adam, as
inferior being, could not have understood. In the first instance, Raphael
steps back to explain a time-eternity assumption (V, 580-582); in the
second he explains celestial change in evening and morning (V, 628-
629); in the third he avoids prolepsis by describing cannon (VI, 573-
575); and in the fourth he briefly reviews heavenly "topography" (VI,
640-641).

Peter's next criticism, that Raphael has edited his tale as to make it
more admonitory by interpolating two lines in the angelic song, is
perhaps the most imperceptive of his suggestions, for it totally fails to
recognize Raphael's admonitory and didactic function in the poem. His
account of the fall of the angels and of the creation is not merely a filler,
a mechanical adherence to the *in medias res* time scheme that demands
recitation of pre-*in medias res* action by a *nuntius*. Like Ulysses'
narration to the Phaeacians, and the princes' narrations to the princesses
in the *New Arcadia*, Raphael's narration is integrally related to the main
action, even in the most literal sense, by its admonitory character. Adam,
not the reader, is the primary audience for Raphael's narration, just as
King Alcinous and the princesses are the primary audiences of the major
restricted narrations of the *Odyssey* and the *New Arcadia* respectively.

---

[13] I distinguish here between the simple and epic simile, the first a normal figure
of speech appropriate to even the most conversational of speeches, the latter extended, formal, highly rhetorical.

God the Father has sent Raphael to warn Adam of impending dangers. To object, therefore, to Raphael's "editing" of his narration is like objecting to the fact of his narrating it. Rather, this editing is a further mark of Milton's deliberate distinction between the two voices.

Peter's criticism of Raphael's use of assertive adjectives as a "debilitating makeshift" is perhaps the most difficult objection to counter, but one which if understood in its larger rhetorical context will further corroborate my contention that Milton is scrupulously aware of the new voice to which he has delegated his narration. By way of introduction to this problem, I shall examine the rhetorical reasons for the peculiar de-emphasis of epic simile in Raphael's narration. The following table will serve as a convenient reference.

Book	Number of Epic Similes	Lines of Omniscient Narration	Dialogue	Delegated Narration
1	14	604	194	–
2	10	489	566	–
5	2	193	359	344
6	2*	–	–	912
7	1*	69	38	553
8	0	66	296	310
9	9	478	707	–

* The only epic similes spoken by Raphael.

First of all, it is obvious that there is some kind of relationship between the frequency of epic simile and the paucity of dialogue and delegated narration. Book I with the highest number of epic similes (14) has also the highest ratio of omniscient narration to dialogue (3 to 1). Book VIII with no epic similes has also the highest ratio of dialogue and delegated narration to omniscient (almost 6 to 1). This phenomenon can be explained on one level, as James Whaler explains it, by the need for "natural propriety" in conversation,[14] a propriety which itself recognizes a clear distinction between types of narrating voice.[15] But on a level of higher rhetoric, the paucity of epic similes in those books dominated by the delegated voice suggests a further awareness of restricted narration scrupulously distinct from the omniscient. Unable to deviate from the high epic style that he has committed himself to and yet recognizing the need for some stylistic mark of distinction between the omniscient and

[14]   James Whaler, "Similes in *Paradise Lost*", *Modern Philology*, XXVIII, 323-326.
[15]   See my comments on the *Iliad* and *Odyssey*, Chapter 2, pp. 50-51.

restricted voices, Milton has invested his own language with an abundance of tropes while denuding Raphael's almost entirely of them. Even on the three occasions when Raphael uses full-blown epic similes,[16] he relates them personally to Adam as his audience and not as independently conceived rhetorical figures:

(1)   As when the total kind
      Of Birds in orderly array on wing
      Came summon'd over Eden *to receive*
      Thir names of thee ...
                                    (VI, 73-77)

(2)   ... *such as to set forth*
      Great things by small, if Nature's concord broke
      Among the constellations war were sprung ...
                                    (VI, 310-315)

(3)   ... as Armies call
      Of Trumpet (*for of Armies thou hast heard*)
      Troop to their standard ...
                                    (VII, 295-297)

Moreover, and most important, Milton's decision to appropriate tropes for his own voice and deny them to the angel is no arbitrary action prompted solely by the need for narrating distinctiveness. In discussing Milton's language, Isabel MacAffrey offers us a reason which, though obviously not intended for our discussion, can easily be accommodated to it.

The conditions of the poem obviously exclude certain poetic devices and styles. ... The typical unit of the Miltonic style cannot be the dramatic image, standing for something else – explicit in allegory, implicit in "oblique" poetry – nor the statement drawing symbolic implication from a concrete presentation, as Wordsworth's verse often does. All these styles, to put the point spectacularly, are styles for a fallen world. All of them are varieties of metaphor, describing an object by comparing it with something else, joining two universes of discourse. Metaphor is a device of rhetoric and dialectic, important ways of explaining and knowing for us, who are obliged to analyze before we can understand. But dialectic itself was one of the unhappy results of the Fall; it is the fallen angels who debate. When the object is completely seen at once, metaphor is unnecessary; it is saturated with the "meaning" that we usually apply to it from the outside.[17]

Now, if the need for metaphor (or trope) is indeed an unhappy condition

---

[16] I count nine similes in Raphael's narration but would identify only three as epic similes. The italics in the three epic similes above are mine.
[17] Isabel MacAffrey, *Paradise Lost as Myth* (Cambridge, Mass., 1959), p. 108.

of fallen nature, it is an *un*necessary verbal device for the intuitive
intelligences of *un*fallen natures, a fact, as we shall see, borne out in
Paradise Lost. The heaviest cluster of tropes (metaphor, simile, highly
imagistic language) is found in the omniscient voice (the omniscient
speaker's own voice is obviously a fallen one) [18] and in the speeches of
the devils. Conversely, the most infrequent recurrence of tropical language is found in Raphael's narration and in the theological dialogue
between the Father and Son, all representing, obviously, unfallen natures, and all, unfairly, bearing the brunt of criticism attacking Milton
for his stylistic deflation from the high points of Books I and II.[19]

But the most spectacular example of this dichotomy between tropical
and non-tropical language is to be found in the language of Adam. Like
Raphael, Adam, up to the climactic fall in Book IX, is an innocent
creature, sharing in the preternatural gifts bestowed upon him by God
and living the same life of grace as Raphael. Their conversation, then,
tends to be bare of tropes and essentially abstract. Even at the brink of
cataclysmic decision, Adam's language is characterized by a clearly un-
metaphorical strain. Note the declamatory diction:

> O fairest of Creation, last and best
> Of all God's Works, Creature in whom excell'd
> Whatever can to sight or thought be form'd,
> Holy, divine, good, amiable, or sweet!
> How art thou lost, how on a sudden lost,
> Defac't, deflower'd, and now to Death devote?
> Rather how hast thou yielded to transgress
> The strict forbiddance, how to violate
> The sacred Fruit forbidden! some cursed fraud
> Of enemy hath beguiled thee, yet unknown,
> And mee with thee hath ruined; for with thee
> Certain my resolution is to Die.
>
>   (IX, 896 ff.)

Only *defac't* and *deflower'd* remotely suggest the image word; the rest
of the language, though powerful in its rhetoric, is clearly un-imagistic.

But upon eating the fruit, indulging in "amorous" play and waking
from a sin-induced sleep, Adam shifts the vehicle of his language from
the abstract to the tropical. I underline the obvious examples:

---

[18]   Anne Davidson Ferry's description of the speaker as a fallen man and yet as
an inspired seer "whose divine illumination transcends the limits of mortal vision"
is appropriate here. See *Milton's Epic Voice*, p. 28.
[19]   I come to these observations independently of Mrs. Ferry whose book appeared after these pages were written. See *Milton's Epic Voice*, p. 70 ff. See also
Thomas Greene, *The Descent from Heaven* (New Haven, 1963), pp. 383-387.

O Eve, in evil hour thou didst *give ear*
To that *false Worm*, of whomsoever taught
To counterfeit Man's voice, true in our Fall,
False in our promis'd Rising, since *our Eyes*
Op'n'd we find indeed, and find we know
Both Good and Evil, Good lost, and Evil got,
Which *leaves us naked* thus, of Honor void,
Of Innocence, of Faith, of Purity,
Our wonted Ornaments now soil'd and stain'd. ...
Even shame, *the last of evils*; of the first
Be sure then. How shall I *behold the face*
Henceforth of God or Angel, erst with joy
And rapture so oft beheld? those heav'nly shapes
Will dazzle now this earthly, with thir blaze
Insufferably bright. O might I here
In solitude *live savage*, in *some glade*
Obscur'd, where *highest Woods impenetrable*
To Star or Sun-light, spread thir umbrage broad,
And brown as Evening: Cover me ye pines,
Ye Cedars, with innumerable boughs
Hide me, where I may never see them more. ...
Some tree whose *broad smooth Leaves together sew'd*
And girded on our loins, may cover round
Those middle parts, that this now comer, Shame,
There sit not, and reproach us as unclean.

(IX, 1067-1098)

Most spectacular is Adam's use of the appositional metaphor, the added layer of meaning, in phrases like *our wonted ornaments soil'd and stain'd* which are apposite to Innocence, Faith and Purity; *the last of evils* apposite to shame; and *this new comer* again apposite to shame. In each of these instances, one can recognize the fallen consciousness struggling for the right word, for the necessary analogy to enlighten a benumbed intelligence. And because Adam speaks to us as well as to Eve, we hear him more clearly when he speaks in tropes rather than schematicized rhetoric. The fallen Adam is one of us.[20]

---

[20] Kester Svendsen recognizes the change in Adam's epithets toward Eve after the fall but offers little but the obvious explanation that they have become "invective and accusatory". Actually, the heavy tropical significance of the "post-fall" epithets that he catalogues ("thou Serpent", "a rib crooked by nature", "this noveltie on earth") contrasts against the less than tropical "pre-fall" epithets ("my espous'd Eve", "my ever new delight" "my other self", "fairest this of all thy gifts", "sole Eve", "above all living creatures deare"). Only "bone of my bone" and "flesh of my flesh" of the epithets he lists here tend to the tropical, but even these are more traditional formulas for Eve than striking tropes. See "Epic Address and Reference in *Paradise Lost*", *Philological Quarterly*, XXVIII, 191.

If I may return then to Peter's criticism of Raphael's use of assertive adjectives by way of this long introduction, it seems that the problem answers itself. Raphael's special use of these adjectives bespeaks not a "debilitating makeshift" but rather a subtle Miltonic attempt to characterize a distinctive voice in the only way open to him. The fallen poet, though lifted by divine inspiration, speaks a highly tropical, and more human, language to his readers who share his fallen state. The unfallen angel speaks a highly rhetorical, less tropical, and less human language to his unfallen audience who up to this point at least is in no need of metaphor.

The preceding analysis has been an attempt to prove Milton's conscious and artistic delegation of his omniscience to a restricted narrator in Books V through VIII. If any arguments can be marshalled against this contention, they would probably be recruited from the area of Raphael's restricted knowledge, that is, the relationship between what he clearly knows and what he reports to Adam. It has been indicated in the discussions of both the *Odyssey* and the *New Arcadia* that the omniscient narrator never gives away his omniscience to a restricted voice without in some way accounting for the source of what the new voice is narrating. Most of the time, of course, the new voice simply reports what action he himself has participated in, but in some instances the action takes place outside of the experiences of the limited consciousness. Ulysses' experience with Circe and with Hyperion's disposition of his men who slaughtered the Sun Cattle is an appropriate example. So is Queen Helen's account (in the *New Arcadia*) of Amphialus's whereabouts and Basilius's version of Erona's sad fate.

In *Paradise Lost*, this problem of the narrator's story extending beyond his source of knowledge is complicated by the fact that an archangel is narrator. Even granting the necessary limiting of angelic knowledge for dramatic purposes, it is obvious that Milton considers an angel to know more than a man. The question is: how much more? In attempting to corroborate my contention that Raphael's function as limited narrator is not to be confused with the omniscient voice's function, I have checked every item of Raphael's narration against the clear source of knowledge of what he is reporting. The results, for the most part, support my contention, but there remain a few inconsistencies.

I have distinguished among those events which Raphael reports that are: 1) clearly *within* his knowledge, 2) *conjecturally within* his knowledge, and 3) *ostensibly outside* his knowledge. Those events clearly within his knowledge I would classify as:

a. The whole of the account of Creation except for the particulars of Adam's creation. With Uriel, Gabriel and Michael, Raphael is one of the four angels of the Presence; and when Uriel informs Satan in Book III that "I saw when at his Word the formless Mass/ This world's material mould, came to a heap," (III, 708-709) we can assume that Raphael too witnessed the creative act, particularly when he describes the angelic rejoicing in Heaven after God the Father announces his intention to create the world (VII, 154-173). Our assumption is strengthened when Raphael specifically informs Adam that on the day he was created God assigned him and a band of other angels to a special mission, (VIII, 229 ff.) a bit of information that not only makes Adam's narration meaningful but also implies Raphael's obvious knowledge of the creation that preceded.

b. The Heavenly Consult at which the Father announces his Son's vice-gerency (V, 577-615). Raphael would have known this by his very presence among "th' Empyrical Host/ Of Angels by Imperial summon call'd" (V, 583-585).

c. The Father's knowledge of Satan's treachery (though not the specifics of the treachery itself) (V, 711 ff.). Again, Raphael would have known this by his continued presence at the celestial throne; he and the three other angels of the Presence are especially privy to God's decrees.

d. The heavenly mobilization for war (VI, 19-413) and the battle on the second day at which the Son defeats the Devils. Raphael, as one of the combatants, would have a soldier's knowledge of the events;[21] moreover, Raphael specifically makes mention of his observation:

> Messiah his triumphal Chariot turn'd:
> To meet him all his saints, who silent stood
> Eye-witnesses of his Almighty Acts.
> (VII, 881-883)

Of those events "conjecturally" within his knowledge, I would include:

a. Satan's consult at which Raphael is obviously not present (V, 869 ff.). It seems to me here that the episode of the faithful Abdiel (in answer to David Daiches' petulant question: what was Abdiel doing among Satan's host anyway?)[22] is reported not only for the importance of his exemplary loyalty but also as a source of knowledge for the events that took place at the rebel's consult. The fact that Abdiel is expected to report the "tidings" seems to be Milton's attempt at explaining Raphael's

---

[21] Raphael's only reference to himself in battle occurs at VI, 362 ff.
[22] *A Critical History of English Literature* (New York, 1960), p. 443.

knowledge of events that he could not directly have known by himself. Satan sneers thus at the faithful Abdiel:

> This report,
> These tidings carry to th'anointed King;
> And fly, ere evil intercept thy flight.
>
> (V, 869-871)

b. Also explainable in a similar manner is Raphael's account of Satan's decision in the second synod (VI, 414-523) to use gunpowder against the heavenly host. Again, Raphael's intimate knowledge of the proceedings can be explained by the advance report of Zophiel (his name means the *spy* of God) whose presence at line 535 seems to serve no other function. Yet, it must be admitted that Raphael's knowledge of the proceedings of the second synod through Zophiel's instrumentality is obviously not so nearly convincing as Raphael's knowledge of the proceedings of the first synod at which Abdiel was clearly a participant.[23] Zophiel's function here seems more a scout's than an immediate observer's. Moreover, the peculiar inference in each instance that despite Abdiel's and Zophiel's reports the heavenly host already know what to expect [24] suggests that perhaps it was their proximity to the throne of God that kept them in knowledge and not any other "source". Raphael's commentary on the Eternal eye [25] seems to corroborate this probability. Moreover, Milton's description of the heavenly host gathering around the Celestial Throne to hear God's explanation of Man's fall is dramatically suggestive of the way angelic knowledge was received and divine knowledge dispensed (X, 26-34).

c. Indeed, the Eternal eye is the only explanation for the single event

---

[23] Alan H. Gilbert's explanation of Abdiel's place in the synod is not entirely satisfactory. He says that "part of the force of the seraph's conduct lies in its initial improbability. ... If the story of Abdiel had been omitted, the quality of the poem would be lower, but the plot would not appear in any sense lacking." "The Theological Basis of Satan's Rebellion and the Function of Abdiel in *Paradise Lost*", *Modern Philology*, XL, 40.

[24]   War he perceiv'd, war in procinct, and found
       Already known what he for news had thought
       To have reported.
>
>   (VI, 19-22)

[25]   Meanwhile th'Eternal eye, whose sight discerns
       Abstrusest thoughts, from forth his holy Mount
       And from within the golden Lamps that burn
       Nightly before him saw without thir light
       Rebellion rising, saw in whom, how spread
       Among the sons of Morn, what multitudes
       Were banded to oppose his high decree.
>
>   (V, 711 ff.)

that seems totally outside Raphael's knowledge. Satan's envious reaction to the Father's commendation of his Son at the Heavenly Consult and Satan's clandestine command to Beelzebub to assemble his hosts (V, 673-693) cannot be explained in any other way, if indeed they can be explained "away" at all. Perhaps it would be more honest to say here that Milton in this instance simply failed to attribute a source of knowledge to his restricted narrator and momentarily slipped back into the style of the omniscient narrator.[26]

3

An item of importance in the preceding chapters on Homer and Sidney centered on the need for a dramatic motivation for the delegation of voice from omniscience to restriction and, after the delegated story has been told, on the need for a "causal" movement back to the main action. Or, in terms of epic criticism: incident must lead dramatically into episode, and episode (with its own speaker or speakers and special internal audience) itself forward the course of the main action. The *Odyssey* was found to be brilliantly handled in this regard, Ulysses' story to the Phaeacians serving both the past needs (exposition) of the main action and affecting the subsequent incidents themselves. That is

---

[26] Gilbert explains this and what he considers to be other inconsistencies by suggesting that the narratives of the fifth, sixth and seventh books were originally placed in chronological order. Thus, after the invocation and statement of subject came the war in Heaven (Books IV and V); and after the account of Satan's host in hell and his voyage (Books I and II) came the account of the Creation (Book VII). Because Milton, at this stage in the development of the poem, did not use an *in medias res* time arrangement, he did not need a character as narrator, but recounted the entire epic in the omniscient voice. When, however, he decided to pattern his epic after the *Odyssey*, he transferred the account of the action preceding Satan's defeat to Raphael, and in some instances failed to make the necessary revisions. As attractive as this hypothesis is, it strains somewhat at self-justification. Gilbert reads passages such as: "for who, though with the tongue/ Of Angels, can relate ... that may lift/ Human imagination to such highth/ Of Godlike power" and "I might relate of thousands, and thir names/ Eternize here on earth ..." as examples of "unrevision" in which Milton, rather than Raphael, is the speaker. But the voice can just as easily be interpreted as Raphael's, the "human imagination" in the first passage being Adam's and the "here on earth" being Eden. At any rate, Gilbert's hypothesis complements my contention that Milton is conscious of the necessary distinction between voices if only by saying that there resulted some failures of revision when the account was transferred to Raphael. To identify *some* failures of revision is to admit that by and large the revisions were successful. If Gilbert is right, the effect on my thesis is no more destructive than the fact of Sidney's revision. The important consideration, then, is not whether the finished product represents a revision, but rather whether or not the revision works. For Gilbert's hypothesis, see *On the Composition of Paradise Lost* (Chapel Hill, 1947), Chapter III.

to say, Ulysses is afforded the opportunity to tell his story in the first place because the main action modulated into it properly, and he finally returns to Ithaca because he has narrated the story to a sympathetic audience. The major delegated narrations in the *New Arcadia* also function in a similar way. Pamela finally marries Musidorus and Philoclea marries Pyrocles because the stories of the two princes stir the affections of the princesses.[27]

To what extent can *Paradise Lost* be measured in this way? There is no question that the dramatic motivation of both the major and minor delegated narrations is successfully handled. The archetypal after-dinner speech which we saw in Ulysses' narration to the Phaeacians, Aeneas's to Dido, and even Kalander's to Musidorus, is also utilized in *Paradise Lost*. But there are a number of reasons why, like Ulysses' situation and unlike Aeneas's, the episodes are not adventitious to the main action, but closely connected.[28] Raphael has been commissioned by God to seek out Adam and to warn him of the impending dangers in order to frustrate Satan's design on mankind. Thus, every bit of information that Raphael reveals of the fall in Heaven and of the creation is ordained to an admonitory, as well as expository, end. Adam must fully realize the nature of his antagonist, or any conflict between man and devil would be grossly unfair. To make Raphael's revelation dramatically appropriate, Milton sketches Adam as curiously ignorant of a number of things that he must appreciate not only to be equally matched with his antagonist but also to be fully culpable for his sin. Although the fact of Adam's ignorance is theologically questionable, it is dramatically effective, for the worst kind of exposition is one in which the expositor informs his audience at length about things of which he is fully aware. Adam's unabashed curiosity, therefore, must be related to what he does not know; and the areas of ignorance that have been clarified should be related, by all the norms of dramatic propriety, to what ultimately causes his downfall.

In the course of the main action immediately preceding Raphael's

---

[27] Although the marriages are not realized in the *New Arcadia* because the work was never finished, there is no doubt that the resolution of the *Old Arcadia*, in which the marriages actually take place, would also have been followed here.

[28] Dr. Johnson, in a critical aside, has already suggested this. "Of episodes", he writes in *The Lives of the Poets*, "there are only two, contained in Raphael's relation of the war in Heaven and Michael's porphetick account of the changes to happen in this world. Both are closely connected with the great action; one was necessary to Adam as a warning, the other as a consolation." *Selected Prose and Poetry*, ed. Bertrand Bronson (New York, 1952), p. 457.

narration, Adam cursorily reveals three items of ignorance that relate directly to his ultimate sin. The first occurs after Eve's evil dream at which time Adam tries to reassure her of her inculpability by denying the possibility of her harboring any evil. It is as if he is saying that her will has been fixed in goodness, and deviation from it impossible.

> This uncouth dream of evil sprung I fear;
> Yet evil whence? in thee can harbor none,
> Created pure.
>
> (V, 99-101)

The second occurs when Raphael admonishes Adam and Eve to obedience, and Adam replies (with more pious emotion than thought) that gratitude in them for their having been created in the first place would necessarily insure obedience, that disobedience is impossible.

> But say,
> What meant that caution join'd, *if ye be found*
> *Obedient*? can we want obedience then
> To him, or possibly his love desert
> Who form'd us from the dust, and plac'd us here
> Full to the utmost measure of what bliss
> Human desires can seek or apprehend?
>
> (V, 512-518)

In both these instances, Adam reveals a dangerous lack of self-knowledge, not to mention a certain presumptuous assurance of his own moral strength. It is not until Raphael explains the nature of free will that Adam admits his ignorance of this truth, a startling admission for the Father of mankind and one that would probably never hold up in any theological "court of law", but an admission of ignorance that clearly motivates Raphael to proceed to his narration "for thy good ... dispens't".

If the episode has been clearly prepared for and successfully modulated into, what of the relationship of episode to subsequent incident? Is Raphael's story, like Aeneas's to Dido or like Calasiris's to Cnemon in the *Aethiopica*, invested with only expository importance or does the narration of the episode itself affect the course of the main plot? Heliodorus utterly failed to tie episode to incident because Cnemon, the audience of Calasiris's story of Chariclea and Theagenes, drops out of the main action shortly after he hears the story. Virgil succeeded only partially in this respect by directing Aeneas's account of the fall of Troy at Dido who also is removed from the action shortly after the narration.[29]

---

[29] The love affair, however, does dramatize the sacrifice of Aeneas's mission by his very abnegation of it.

But Raphael's delegated narration serves more than the obvious needs of exposition. First, it clearly supplies in Adam those dangerous intellectual defects that might have left him inculpable of the "mortal sin original" he is to commit. That Adam has understood Raphael's teaching unequivocally is later made clear in his warning to the recalcitrant Eve who had refused to praise a fugitive and cloistered virtue and the recognition in Book XII of his own human limitations:

> Greatly instructed I shall hence depart,
> Greatly in peace of thought, and have my fill
> Of knowledge, what this vessel can containe;
> Beyond which was my folly to aspire.
>
> (XII, 557-560)

> God left free the Will, for what obeys
> Reason, is free, and Reason he made right,
> But bid her well beware, and still erect,
> Lest by some fair appearing good surpris'd
> She dictate false, and misinform the Will
> To do what God expressly hath forbid.
>
> (IX, 351-356)

Furthermore, and more important, it seems that by Adam's almost obtuse reaction to the angel's story – Raphael having stressed the importance of knowledge for the sake of *moral* perfection [30] and Adam inquiring merely after an answer to the Ptolemaic-Copernican controversy – Raphael's initiating of his audience into the "mysteries" of higher knowledge has only succeeded in whetting Adam's appetite for more. The decline of licit attitudes in Adam toward divine revelation following upon each item of Raphael's narration dramatizes this point.[31] After Raphael has concluded his story of the War in Heaven, Adam thanks the "Divine Interpreter" as messenger, and God as message-sender, for having forewarned him of the impending dangers and requests an account of creation in order that man's knowledge might "the more magnify his [God's] works" (VII, 96). But upon hearing Raphael complete the account of creation, Adam wants to hear more. Forgetting the expressed admonitory intention of Raphael's narrative and even for

---

[30]   Raphael's warning and Adam's seeking knowledge for its own sake are well dramatized at VII, 625 to VIII, 38.

[31]   Harold E. Toliver explains Adam's obtuseness thusly: "Every word Raphael speaks to Adam, ostensibly to lessen the distance between God and man, only widens that distance, for, despite their accurate labelling of each other and their friendship, there is more respect than love between them." "Complicity of Voice in *Paradise Lost*", *Modern Language Quarterly*, XXV, 168.

the moment putting off the *pro-gloria-Dei* sentiments, Adam profusely thanks the "Divine Historian" for having "*largely* . . . allayed/ The thirst I had of knowledge". Whereupon he confesses that "something yet of doubt remains" and immediately proceeds, with little attempt at justifying his curiosity, into his questions about astronomical phenomena, an inquiry obviously unrelated to the admonitory or God-glorifying intention of the previous two requests. This aspiration to higher scientific knowledge for its own sake seems at least seminally related to Adam's later sinful justification of his sin:

> He [the serpent] yet lives,
> Lives, as thou saids't, and gains to live as Man
> Higher degree of Life, inducement strong
> To us, as likely tasting to attain
> Proportional ascent, which cannot be
> But to be Gods, or Angels Demi-Gods.
> (IX, 932-937)

Raphael's narration with its limited revelation of knowledge proper to Adam's needs, therefore, relates to the main action by ironically producing in Adam not the expected intellectual attitude of "lowly wise" but the desire to "attain proportional ascent . . . to be Gods". Thus, the pattern of God's designs on his Creation suffers a further frustration: the Divine means of admonition, the channels of mercy and grace, Man corrupts into an occasion of sin.

The modulation into the minor delegated narration and that narration's "causal" relationship to the subsequent incident is also brilliantly handled. Milton allows Adam to relate his own experiences on the day of his creation for a number of reasons. First, Adam incidates that he wishes to tell his story because he desires to detain the angelical visitor whose "discourse is [sweeter] to my ear/ Than Fruits of Palm-Tree pleasantest to thirst" (VIII, 211-212). This enforced hospitality seems to be only half the reason, as we shall see later. Second, Raphael, being the gracious guest, indicates that he would like to hear Adam's story because he was not a witness to this highest of God's creative acts. He was "that Day . . . absent . . . Bound on a voyage . . . toward the gates of Hell/ To see that none thence issu'd forth a spy" (VIII, 229 ff.). But even this reason sounds curiously accommodating on Raphael's part. The angel "volunteers" a reason for Adam's narration which Adam himself did not require.

Actually, the modulation into the minor delegated narrative is closely related to the impact of the story on subsequent events in the main

action. In his narration, Adam reveals to Raphael an almost uncon-
scious uxoriousness that, along with his desire to "attain proportional
ascent", represents Adam's tragic flaw. And whether this uxoriousness is present in his character before he actually articulates his feelings
for Eve is only of secondary importance in this discussion. Granted
Milton's "anticipating the Fall by attributing to Eve and Adam feelings
which though nominally felt in the state of innocence are actually not
compatible to it".[32] The fact remains that this is Adam's first opportunity
to reveal to another rational creature the very human involvement of a
man with his wife; and Adam, after having listened for 1800 lines to
Raphael's unique high argument, is anxious to counter with some
quintessential experiences of his own. That he decides to tell Raphael his
story whether Raphael has heard it or not ("which *perhaps* thou hast not
heard") suggests that it is not the uxoriousness alone that the delegated
narration underscores but the articulation, the definition, of that
uxoriousness as well. Adam knows that Raphael cannot have experienced this "commotion strange" (witness the angel's blush when Adam
questions him about love in Heaven); and Adam has every intention of
making some revelations of his own. Note the disproportion in his
narration between the number of lines devoted to the details of his own
experiences before Eve's creation (107 lines) and the number of those
devoted to the details of her creation and their partnership (203 lines).
Note especially the crescendo of passionate enthusiasm in his narration
which reaches its high point in his hyperbolic description of her beauties:
"so lovely fair/ That what seem'd fair in all the World, seem'd now
Mean" (VIII, 471-473). "All higher knowledge in her presence falls/
Degraded, Wisdom in discourse with her/ Loses discount'nanc't, and like
folly shows" (VIII, 551-553). It is as if Adam's propensity to uxoriousness already active in him becomes stimulated by the very words which
he uses to describe this weakness for the "charm of Beauties powerful
glance".

These last Petrarchan sentiments contract even Raphael's brow and
he reacts with his second serious admonition, the first having enjoined
Adam to be "lowly wise": ". . . fair no doubt, and worthy well/ Thy
cherishing, thy honoring, and thy love/ Not thy *subjection*" (VIII, 568-
570, italics mine). Again, however, the admonition which Raphael feels
constrained to articulate goes unheeded at the very moment of highest
temptation in Adam; for it is his refusal to live without Eve (when he

[32] E. M. W. Tillyard, *Studies in Milton* (London, 1951), p. 11.

realizes that by her sin he must lose her) that represents the immediate reason for his own participation in the Fall. Thus, the two delegated narrations occasion a reaction in Adam which leads directly to his original sin. Rather than limit and legitimatize Adam's aspiration to high knowledge, Raphael's narration unwittingly hastens the process away from "lowly wise". And rather than define for the angelical visitor his conjugal happiness with his spouse, Adam's narration articulates and intensifies uxorious passions which even the prospect of eternal damnation cannot cool.

4

The direct relationship between episode and incident reviewed in the last section is only part of the total narrative intention occasioned by the delegated voice. We remember that the epic artist does more than utilize the delegated narrative as a device of exposition or as a device by which to forward the main action. Although these functions are significant in their own right, they tend to serve as answers to the exigencies of plot structure only in its most literal sense. Actually, as we saw in both the *Odyssey* and the *New Arcadia*, there exists a relationship between episode and incident, or delegated narration and omniscient narration, that might be described as supra-literal: the relationship of narrative microcosm to macrocosm, of the foreshadowing to the foreshadowed. We saw, for example, that the central motifs in the episodes of the *Odyssey* served as structural parallels to the motifs of the main action: that the adventures which Ulysses experienced paralleled, sometimes literally and sometimes ironically, the incidents of the main action. Thus, the "inhospitality" he received at the hands of his various unwilling hosts served as an ingratiating foil to the hospitality of the Phaeacians and as an ironic foil to Penelope's necessary hospitality to her suitors.

To what extent does the delegated narration of *Paradise Lost* function in this way? Many critics have recognized the elaborate system of structural and thematic balances that Milton worked into his poem: the balance of the infernal and heavenly consults and of the holy and "unholy" trinities; [33] the rhetorical balances in the speeches of the infernal and celestial characters; [34] the extraordinary parallel, in the Son's reply to the Father (III, 150-166), to the pattern of the debate in hell; [35] and,

---

[33] For a brief discussion of this, see Hughes, p. 177.
[34] J. B. Broadbent, "Milton's Rhetoric", *Modern Philology*, LVI, 230.
[35] Florence L. Walzl, "Milton's *Paradise Lost*, III, 150-166", *Explicator*, XX (Oct., 1961), entry 11.

more spectacularly, the bipartite and pyramidic structure of the entire epic that reminds one strongly of Cedric Whitman's similar charting of the structure of the *Iliad*.[36]

A further recognition of balances can be achieved when the critic looks at *Paradise Lost* from the perspective of incident-episode or from the parallels implicit in the omniscient voice-restricted voice narrations, parallels already examined in the *Odyssey* and the *New Arcadia*. I see at least four significant examples of structural and thematic balance in comparing Raphael's narration with the narration of the omniscient speaker. First, it is revelatory of the characters of the original sinners (Satan in Heaven and Adam in Eden) that their offence against God is occasioned in each instance by a revelation which presumably is intended to strengthen them in their obedience. It is true, of course, that the reactions to their individual revelations *seem* different. Satan for example chafes at God the Father's revelation to "th' Empyreal Host"/ ("this day I have begot him I declare/ My only Son. . . . your Head I him appoint") and reacts disloyally to the divine edict whereas Adam seems to accept the admonitions of the angelic messenger. Yet, if my understanding of Adam's sin is correct – that it is not until Raphael delivers the admonition and defines the problem of "lowly wise" and male subjection that Adam's propensities to these moral problems are activated – it becomes clear to me that his sin too is related in a definite way to the fact of revelation. And it is equally clear that Raphael's detailed account of Satan's sinful reaction to the divine edict looks forward to and actually helps to explain Adam's sin. If the paragon of God's creation can turn against Him and take a third of Heaven's Host with him, it is not inconceivable that Man with his inferior intellect and will can do the same thing. Sons of the world may stain when heaven's son staineth.[37]

A second example of thematic and structural balance occasioned by the delegated narration is the similar attempt at justification for sin that we see both in Raphael's account of Satan's rebellion and in Adam himself in Book IX. Both creatures marshall specious arguments to

[36]   John T. Shawcross, "The Balanced Structure of *Paradise Lost*", *Studies in Philology*, LXII (Oct., 1965), 696-718.
[37]   Relative to this relationship is the role of Abdiel as a foil to both Satan and Adam and Eve. Mason Tung reads the Abdiel episode as a "dramatic illustration of the angelic freedom of the will. . . . [and] therefore instrumental in substantiating the positive alternative that angels, like man, are free to stand, even at times when they are under almost overwhelming pressure to fall". "The Abdiel Episode", *Studies in Philology*, LXII (July, 1965), 599.

justify decisions that have already been made and decisions motivated
in reality for selfish reasons. Satan, really jealous of the highest honor
placed on the Son by the Father, argues himself into a kind of angelic
heresy by questioning his own creation by God. Although the speech is
directed to Abdiel, it reads glibly like one Satan has well rehearsed for
any emergency:

> . . . who saw
> When this creation was? remember'st who saw thou
> Thy making, while the Maker gave thee being?
> We know no time when we were not as now;
> Know none before us, self-begot, self rais'd
> By our own quick'ning power, when fatal course
> Had circl'd his full Orb, the birth mature
> Of this our native Heav'n, Ethereal Sons.
> Our puissance is our own . . .
>
> (V, 856-864)

Adam too, once resolved to sin, frantically searches for justifying reasons
and argues himself into temporary human heresy by questioning the
inexorableness and efficacy of God's will:

> But past who can recall, or done undo?
> Not God Omnipotent, nor fate; yet so
> Perhaps thou shalt not Die, perhaps the Fact
> Is not so heinous now, foretasted Fruit,
> Profan'd first by the Serpent, by him first
> Made common and unhallow'd ere our taste;
> Nor yet on him found deadly, he yet lives . . .
>
> (IX, 926-932)

Larger and more significant than either of the previous two parallels is
the balance between the macrocosmic heavenly war following upon
Satan's decision to rebel and the microcosmic "war" in Eden following
upon Adam's sin. Among all the dyslogistics heaped upon Raphael's
account of the celestial war – from Dr. Johnson's calling it "a confusion
of spirit and matter" [38] and "the favourite of children" to John Peter's
wondering "why the battle should have been reported with such fidelity
and at such length" [39] – none has seen the war in Heaven as a foreshadowing of the human conflict that Adam and Eve suffer in Books
IX and X.[40] If C. S. Lewis's simple but not simplistic formula for the theme

[38] *Samuel Johnson, Selected Prose and Poetry*, p. 465.
[39] Peter, p. 79.
[40] J. R. Watson has perhaps overstated his case in claiming that Books VI and
VII are the structural centers of *Paradise Lost*, but he offers interesting reasons

of *Paradise Lost* can be believed – that goodness makes men happy and
evil makes men miserable – then the kinds of unhappiness following
upon the respective evils of Satan's apostasy in Heaven and Adam's sin
in Eden should show some resemblance to each other. And that resemblance is largely symbolic – the "external" war on the plains of Heaven
being a dramatic type of the "internal" war between Adam and Eve and
God in the confines of their souls:

> Love was not in thir looks either to God
> Or to each other, but apparent guilt,
> and shame, and perturbation, and despair,
> Anger, and obstinacy, and hate, and guile.
>
> (X, 111-114)

But there exist more specific parallels than these. Milton himself sees
this spiritual condition as a symbolic war when, after Adam and Eve
spend the fruitless hours in "mutual accusation", he laments that "of
thir vain contest appeared no end", the same kind of comment Raphael
makes after the inconclusive war in Heaven: "horrid confusion heapt/
upon confusion rose: and now all Heav'n Had gone to wrack with ruin
overspread". Also, it is hardly accidental that both "battles" begin with
admonitory, but fruitless, negotiations, Abdiel's in the former and
Raphael's in the latter. Moreover, certain images recur in both accounts
that force the reader into recognizing the heavenly war as a foreshadowing of the latter, or more specifically, as a dramatic, even literal,
representation of it. Immediately following upon his sin, for example,
Adam, with more rhetorical than literal supplication, calls upon the
woods to "spread their umbrage broad": "Cover me ye Pines,/ Ye
Cedars, with innumerable boughs." In the Heavenly War, the "sinners"
are *literally* covered:

> From thir foundations loos'ning to and fro
> They pluckt the seated Hills with all thir load,
> Rocks, Waters, Woods, and by the shaggy tops
> Uplifting bore them in thir hands. ...
>   ... and all thir confidence
> Under the weight of Mountains buried deep.
>
> (VI, 644 ff.)

---

nonetheless: "These two books contain the theme of good which is brought out
of evil treated on the grandest scale: Raphael describes the battle in Heaven to
Adam with an epic magnificence, but in Book VII he goes on to outline the great
consequence of this, the Creation." "Divine Providence and the Structure of *Paradise Lost*", *Essays in Criticism*, XIV, 153.

At the confrontation between Adam, Eve, and God, God anathematizes the serpent with the Biblical, metaphorical, curse: "her seed shall bruise they head." Before the heavenly battle, Abdiel had anathematized Satan as "alienate from God", spreading "contagion" and warning him that the "Golden Sceptre which thou didst reject/ Is now an Iron Rod to *bruise* and break/ Thy disobedience . . . soon expect to feel/ His thunder on thy *head*." Which curse turns to actual literal fact when in the battle Abdiel is the first to strike:

> . . . a noble stroke he lifted high
> Which hung not, but so swift with tempest fell
> On the *proud Crest* of Satan.
>
> (VI, 189-191)

But the "declaration" of both wars is only as important as their resolutions. And it is in the resolutions that further significant parallels exist. Just as Adam and Eve in the depths of spiritual loss cannot by their own agency revive themselves but must first be lifted to a new understanding of their condition by the justice and mercy of the Son, so in more dramatic and literal terms, the inconclusive war in Heaven can be resolved only by the instrumentality of the Son in "the Chariot of Paternal Deity". And in both instances, it is the Father, recognizing the plight of those whose will He has created free, who sends the Son – in one instance as merciful judge and in another as warrior – to rescue His creatures from the impasse of their own making.

The final significant parallel between the delegated and omniscient narrations occurs in Book VII. At first glance, this book seems to be the least "foreshadowing" of all the episodes. And yet, coming where it does at the peroratory part of Raphael's narration, one would almost think Milton amiss as a poet if he did not place it in an eminent position. It is significant that Milton follows orthodox tradition in ascribing the creative act to the Second Person of the Trinity. In the *Christian Doctrine*, Milton clearly indicates his adherence to the teaching that the Creation was effected through the Son by the Father.[41] And in *Paradise Lost*, Raphael spends a great deal of time describing the work of the Son in creation:

> Meanwhile the Son
> On his great Expedition now appear'd
> Girt with Omnipotence, with Radiance crown'd
> Of majesty Divine, Sapience and Love

---

[41]   I, ii. In Hughes, p. 956.

Immense, and all his Father in him shone.
About his Chariot numberless were pour'd
Cherub and Seraph, Potentates and Thrones . . .
                    Heav'n op'n'd wide
Her ever-during Gates, Harmonious sound
On golden Hinges moving, to let forth
the King of Glory in his powerful Word
And Spirit coming to create new Worlds.
                              (VII, 192 ff.)

The "new Worlds" which Raphael describes the Son as creating in Book
VII are new, however, only *in tempore* and not *per omnia saecula
saeculorum*; for all this creation, it would seem, looks forward only to the
final new creation, the New Jerusalem, that Milton sees when the reign
of Christ triumphs over the world. Michael's revelation to Adam of the
procession of human history is significant only in terms of the role of
Christ in effecting his new kingdom; and Raphael's account of the
Son's "old" creation becomes Milton's way of paying glory to God who,
in the words of the Roman offertory, "hast established the nature of man
in wondrous dignity and even more wondrously has renewed it".[42]

5

A final, though perhaps anti-climactic, word should be said here about
the relationship between delegated narration and characterization. We
cannot expect to find in *Paradise Lost* anything like the subtle differences in character portrayal that result from the omniscient voice's
delegation of its function to the restricted voice or voices in works like
the *Odyssey* or the *New Arcadia*. The reason is obvious. Both of the
restricted narrators in *Paradise Lost*, Raphael in the major narration and
Adam in the minor, are unfallen creatures (Adam's sin, of course, is yet
to be committed) whose state, although it does not save them from the
possibility of ignorance and even error, preserves them from guile or
any other intellectual failing that might set the restricted narrator's
opinions and attitudes at a distance from the omniscient's. Thus, the
possibiliy of irony is all but eliminated; and the reader would expect to
find wherever the restricted narrator is describing the same characters
as the omniscient a kind of echoing of sentiments. Needless to say, both
voices praise the Persons in God; both attack Satan and his cohorts for
their perfidy. And yet, when we examine the degree of eulogy or
dyslogy directed toward the Divine Persons and the fallen angels respec-

[42] "Humanae substantiae dignitatem mirabiliter condidisti, et mirabilius refor-
masti."

tively we find an appropriate intensification of these sentiments in the restricted narration.

Except for his report of the angelical alleluias in Book III, for example, the omniscient speaker's attitude towards the Divine Persons is reverently restrained. He allows only nine lines of descriptive introduction before plunging into an account of the Divine witnessing of Satan's voyage, lines more theologically descriptive than effusively rhetorical:

> Now had th'Almighty Father from above,
> From the pure Empyrean where he sits
> High Thron'd above all highth, bent down his eye,
> His own works and their works at once to view:
> About him all the Sanctities of Heaven
> Stood thick as Stars, and from his sight receiv'd
> Beatitude past utterance; on his right
> The radiant image of his Glory sat,
> His only son . . .
>
> (III, 56-64)

When we compare this to Raphael's intensely laudatory description of the Father and Son to Adam:

> . . . the Father infinite,
> By whom in bliss imbosom'd sat the Son,
> Amidst as from a flaming Mount, whose top
> Brightness had made invisible . . .
>
> (V, 596-599)

and his barrage of eulogistic adjectives for the Son, all within two lines: "calm aspect", "clear Lightning Divine, ineffable, serene", we come to realize that Raphael's represents an unusual degree of honorific characterization.

The reason is probably determined by the presence of Adam as audience in the restricted narration. For his edification, Raphael, as a member of the Empyreal Host closest to God and as a messenger commissioned to advise Adam of his "happy state" and to warn him of his enemy, loads his characterizations of Adam's "friends" with highly assertive praise.

The good characters in Raphael's estimate, therefore, when they are good are very, very good; the bad characters are concomitantly horrid. Compare, for example, the close frequency of assertive adjectives praising the loyal Abdiel ("fervent Angel", "flaming Seraph", "fearless", "faithful only hee/ Among innumerable false, unmov'd/ Unshak'n, unseduc'd, unterrifi'd"; "dreadless", "undaunted") to the equal intensity of the assertive adjectives condemning Satan ("false", "bad", "calumnious", "counterfeited"). Certainly the omniscient voice also uses these adjectives, but seldom in such a highly clustered combination. Indeed, in his attitude toward the Deity, Raphael sounds every bit like a courtier trying to persuade another, by almost hyperbolic praise, of the nobility of his lord; and in his attitude toward Satan like an outraged brother, embarrassed and ashamed to admit that of his kind the foremost should have defected.

By contrast, where Raphael is outgoing and profuse in his estimate of others, he is modest and even anonymous in description of himself. Gilbert uses the fact of Raphael speaking of himself in the third person as proof of Milton's having revised the chronological order of his original version and having neglected to make the necessary corrections when the chronological order was changed to the epic order. This explanation may be correct. But it seems in no way to invalidate the success of Raphael's restricted attempts at characterization, particularly of himself. It is a curious fact, for example, that Raphael, for all his many revelations to Adam, should never have revealed his identity to his earthly host. Adam's varied epithets directed at Raphael indicate this fact clearly: "Divine Instructor", "Divine Interpreter", "Divine Historian", "pure intelligence of Heav'n", "Angel serene", "favorable spirit", "propitious guest" are some of the many different salutations with which Adam greets Raphael, but never with his name. Thus, Raphael's only direct mention of himself in the third person continues the modest anonymity. After he has praised the heroic exploits of Michael and Abdiel on the heavenly battle field, Raphael tells Adam that "in other parts like deeds deserv'd Memorial," and he proceeds to mention briefly the exploits of Gabriel, Uriel and himself, his only explanation for his modesty contained in his statement that "those elect/ Angels contented with thir fame in Heav'n/ Seek not the praise of men." If this modesty has any function beyond that of self-characterization, it can be related to the admonitory quality of Raphael's narration. Uriel and Raphael both vanquish enemies "that to be less than Gods/ disdain'd." The desolate fate of the ambitious angels and the victory of the modest content to be submissive to God warn Adam of the personal cataclysm that is to come in his own soul.

The subtleties of characterization briefly reviewed above, not to mention the host of sophisticated narrative techniques reviewed in the earlier sections, dramatize Milton's unqualified success in adapting to his peculiar needs the convention of *in medias res* narration. Although the correlative device of restricted voice is occasionally strained when it becomes necessary for the omniscient narrator to delegate to an angel instead of a man, Milton is able to satisfy the theological demands of angelic knowledge while at the same time giving Raphael a local habitation and a name. The resulting artistry speaks further tribute to a man in whose hands an ancient narrative technique survives as strongly and vitally as in Homer's own day. The blind has led the blind, and the world of literature has been the brighter.

V. THE FAERIE QUEENE

1

I place *The Faerie Queene* last in the series of English epics to be
examined according to the system outlined above because Spenser alone
of the great English epic writers failed to appreciate or take advantage
of the innumerable narrative strategies resulting from a commitment to
an *in medias res* structure. Although neither Sidney nor Milton slavishly
imitated their Homeric prototype in this regard, both men nevertheless
exploited in their own way the relationship existing between *in medias
res* structure and restricted voice. Spenser, despite his extraordinary
talents in other areas of narrative, did not.

My analysis of his defects in this technique, however, will not demean
Spenser's accomplishments on the level of allegory. The penetrating work
of a number of recent scholars [1] in charting the intricacies of Spenser's
allegory has indicated that he was a sensitive artist who by his "darke
conceits" judged and dramatized human experience at a level of complexity that no allegorist in English literature had been able to reach.
But in those areas of literal narrative most obviously touched by the *in
medias res* tradition, Spenser's decision to build an *in medias res* structure while constructing above it upper stories of allegory was not a happy
one. This is not to say that the allegory suffered any rude shocks, but it
is to say that the demands of allegory on the literal narrative beneath it
made any sophisticated functioning of the *in medias res* strategies there
all but impossible.

The reason for this difficulty is that there exists an almost inherent

---

[1] Harry Berger, Jr., *The Allegorical Temper* (New Haven, 1957); M. Pauline
Parker, *The Allegory of the Faerie Queene* (Oxford, 1960); A. C. Hamilton,
Allegory in The Faerie Queene (Oxford, 1961); Graham Hough, *A Preface to
The Faerie Queene* (London, 1962); William Nelson, *The Poetry of Edmund
Spenser* (New York, 1963); Thomas P. Roche, Jr., *The Kindly Flame: A Study of
The Third and Fourth Books of Spenser's Faerie Queene* (Princeton, 1964).

contradiction between the thematic demands of allegory and some of the necessary narrative by-products of the *in medias res* narration. Allegory, by its very nature, tends away from doubts and uncertainties, from an enunciation of ambiguous and ambivalent truths, and works toward the explicit theme, albeit in a mode that is polysemous.[2] Allegory does not delight in paradox or irony or indulge in irresolvable questions. But because its nature is essentially foliate or laminated,[3] allegory can be manipulated only by a narrator who is consciously and at all times in control of its often unwieldy operations. And because its intention is essentially didactic, the allegorical mode cannot chance its mission to a voice that does not speak with omniscient authority.

As we have seen in the previous chapters, however, one necessary correlative of the *in medias res* structure is the restricted narrator returning to relate those episodes prerequisite to the main action. And for the restricted narrator to function successfully within that tradition, he must exploit those areas of narration most suited to his particular voice: namely, irony, oblique characterization, ambiguity and tonal ambivalence. The devices by which a restricted narrator would operate most successfully are the very devices that would militate, by their simultaneous presence in a work, against the thematic demands of allegory. In *The Faerie Queene*, therefore, Spenser is being pulled in two opposite directions. On the one hand is his intention "to fashion a gentleman or noble person in vertuous and gentle discipline" by means of "a continued Allegory, or darke conceit"; and on the other is his desire to observe the conventions of the epic poem by "thrusting into the middest ... and there recoursing to the thinges forepaste". The results, on the narrative level, are not always happy.

Wherein do these failures lie? Certainly they do not appear in the area of omniscient narration which by its very nature is a fit instrument for the manipulation of the multi-leveled machinery proper to allegory. Indeed, Spenser's successes in joining the narrative base to the allegorical superstructure occur while the omniscient voice is in full command. But when Spenser tries to answer to the demands of *in medias res* by working with restricted narration, some serious difficulties occur.

Most noticeable of these difficulties is the very imbalance that results from the length of omniscient narration on the one hand and the brevity of restricted flashback on the other. Only 30 of the 562 stanzas in Book

[2] For a briefly enunciated contrary view, see Roche, p. 31.
[3] Edward A. Bloom, "The Allegorical Principle", *Journal of English Literary History*, XVIII (Sept., 1951), 163-190.

I, for example, are devoted to the necessary expository narration, or less than six per cent. Book II follows a lesser ratio. Only 29 of its 683 stanzas can be considered as significant restricted exposition, or less than five per cent. Compared to the *Odyssey*, in which more than sixteen per cent of the total narration utilizes the restricted voice, or to *Paradise Lost*, where approximately twenty per cent of the poem is written in restricted voice, *The Faerie Queene* offers a meager harvest indeed.

The results of such an imbalance are as interesting as the reasons for it. On the literal level, exposition suffers because brevity of delegated narration deprives the reader of satisfying his natural curiosity about the backgrounds of the various heroes. Our questions about Red Cross, to use one of the questors as an example, are only partially answered. Of course, we realize that on the allegorical level he represents Everyman embarking on a spiritual odyssey towards holiness and that his objective adventures represent the spiritual obstacles and reverses inherent in such a quest. But if his odyssey is to be humanly and complexly motivated, the demands of exposition on the narrative level must be satisfied. Who is this "gentle knight . . . pricking on the plaine"? What about his mother and father, or his friends at Gloriana's court, or his exploits before he arrived there? Certainly, Spenser's assertion that Red Cross was a male Cinderella whets our appetite for the details of his transformation. Yet, Spenser seems reluctant to allow his hero, or even an observer of the hero's action, to divulge at any length the details of his background.

The reasons for this reluctance are rooted in the contradiction between allegory and *in medias res* described earlier. Having begun his action in the middle with a necessary minimum of exposition, Spenser was forced to return to the expository action later in the book by means of a *nuntius*. But because the demands of his allegory could not be reconciled to the subtleties of a restricted narrator's function, Spenser allowed the narrator (in this case, Una) only enough of a story as the successful execution of his allegory would allow. As we shall see later, Una's few stanzas about Red Cross are simply not enough.

Other blemishes, raised by the above problem, are also observable. Because of the allegory-inhibited brevity of restricted narration, the functional relationship of episode to incident is all but eliminated in *The Faerie Queene*. Under ordinary circumstances, a first-person narration of an earlier action, in addition to supplying the necessary exposition, functions as an integral and not adventitious force on the *subsequent* action. This study has repeatedly demonstrated that Ulysses' story supplies more than the mere expository details of his storm-wracked voyages from Troy to Phaeacia. By working on the sensitivities of his auditors, Ulysses' recitation excites them emotionally into offering him convoy to Ithaca. The *New Arcadia* and *Paradise Lost* utilize a similar kind of dramatic situation. But in the various restricted narrations of *The Fairie Queene*, no such "forwarding" movement results. In Guyon's case, to use the example of another knight of Gloriana's court, his revelation to Medina of the details of his quest (II, ii, 40-44) is in no way connected to his ultimate arrival at or destruction of the Bower of Bliss. Nor, for that matter, is Una's revelation to Arthur of the details of the Red Cross knight's quest related directly to his ultimate slaying of the dragon.[4] In both of these examples, the audience is simply not significant enough an element in the story's structure. In the *Odyssey* the audience to Ulysses' story are the Phaeacians; in the *New Arcadia* the audience to the princes' stories are the princesses themselves; in *Paradise Lost* the audience to Raphael's story is Adam. But in *The Faerie Queene* the audiences to the various restricted narrations are characters who either do not participate in, or do not significantly help to effect the resolution of, the main action. Medina, for example, disappears from Book II after she hears Guyon's story. The fact that Spenser selected her house as the setting for Guyon's story and her person as the audience for it is, for all practical purposes, a wasted motion and, except for the very mechanical device of his leaving Amavia's child in her care, a non-functional detail.

Another weakness resulting from the structural incompatibility of *in medias res* with the allegorical mode can be detected in the perfunctory quality of the delegated speakers' voices. It often seems that Spenser is affording only token recognition to the integrity of the delegated speaker and failing to give up his own omniscience once he has committed himself to such a delegation. With the possible exception of Raphael's account of Satan's first consult in Book V of *Paradise Lost*, the epic writers already analyzed scrupulously followed the lead of Homer in the *Odyssey* in granting Ulysses full autonomy in the telling of his story. This autonomy relates to such diverse considerations as the epistemological integrity of the delegated narrator: never revealing material

---

[4] One might object that if Una had not told her story to Arthur (I, vii, 42-52) he would not have come to Red Cross's aid and slain Orgoglio; but even in this regard the telling of the story has only an indirect relationship to Red Cross's ultimate confrontation with the dragon. Furthermore, since it is Arthur's function to intervene in each of the quests, his coming to Red Cross's aid is really not contingent upon Una's telling of the story. Any wayfarer informing Arthur of Orgoglio's dungeon would have effected the same response.

beyond his ability to know it, and the stylistic decorum of the new voice: the appropriateness of rhetorical patterns to the character of the speaker.[5] With Spenser, however, the distinctions rehearsed above are often blurred. Una narrates her story and Guyon his and a host of other characters theirs, but one hears nothing particularly distinctive in their voices.

Here again the incompatibility of allegory and *in medias res* reveals itself. In Una's case, for example, it is fitting that as an allegorical representation of truth her words take on a certain omniscient quality. And in those large areas of omniscient narration where her only speeches are part of the dialogue controlled by the omniscient voice, it is altogether proper that this allegorical demand be met. But when, because of the structural need for a return to prerequisite action by a narrator, Una is forced into the temporary role of delegated speaker, the quasi-omniscience proper to her in her allegorical *persona* no longer fits. Suddenly her explanations which ascribe the failure of earlier knights in killing the dragon to their lack of faith or guilt of sin, for example, sound a great deal like an intrusion, like an omniscient author paying no attention to the restriction of his delegated speaker's knowledge:

> Yet never any could that girlond win,
> But all still shronke, and still he greater grew:
> All they for want of faith, or guilt of sin,
> The pitteous pray of his fierce crueltie have bin.
>
> (I, vii, 45)

Even her explanation of the dragon's hellish origins – "bred in the loathly lakes of Tartary" – seems curiously inappropriate to the limited knowledge forced upon her by the demands of the *in medias res* structure. And if the statement is intended as rhetorical formality and not literal fact, one's feelings are that on the simple narrative level, which cannot be dissociated from the *in medias res* demands of this particular scene, such rhetoric in a young maiden lamenting the fate of her beloved is equally out of place. Had the same lament been narrated omnisciently, it would have been easily accommodated to her nature on its many levels.

This kind of rhetorical display, effective when it is handled by the omniscient narrator, fails unequivocally when it comes from Spenser's

---

[5] We saw, for example, that Sidney carefully accounted for every item of knowledge that his delegated voices narrated, that Milton carefully distinguished between the powerful tropical poetry of his own omniscient voice and the more abstract rhetorical poetry of Raphael's restricted, but unfallen, voice.

characters. The very fact, indeed, that Spenser allows epic allusion in the voice of a restricted narrator further suggests that, despite the delegation of omniscience to various characters throughout *The Faerie Queene*, he had never been able to surrender to the new delegated speaker the prerogatives of omniscient voice. To hear Amavia introduce an epic allusion to Cynthia while in the throes of death, for example, indicates to me that, despite the mechanical adherence to the demands of *in medias res*, no genuine delegation has taken place.

> Now had fayre Cynthia by even tournes
> Full measured three quarters of her yeare,
> And thrise three tymes had fild her crooked hornes.
> (II, ii, 52)

One might appreciate the appropriateness of the time and chastity symbols in this allusion, particularly as they relate to a situation in which a man's time has run out because of unchastity, if the epic allusion had been voiced by the omniscient narrator. But coming in the last breaths of the dying Amavia, the allusion seems a mere mouthing of the omniscient voice's part in another key and not, as it should have been, a new tone from an entirely different instrument.

These scattered examples of the failure of restricted voice in *The Faerie Queene* underscore Spenser's problem. *In medias res*, with its necessary delegation of story to a speaker or speakers inside the work, demands a realistic or quasi-realistic handling of characters and incidents wherever restricted voice controls the course of the narrative. Although allegory demands for its successful execution an acute awareness of the real problems of human experience, its multi-leveled machinery tends to exclude the realistic mode. One or the other had to suffer in *The Faerie Queene*. Spenser chose to be a successful allegorist.

2

An examination of the individual books of *The Faerie Queene* will reveal that Spenser, for all his honorific attention to the *in medias res* epic tradition in his prefatory letter to Raleigh, recognized the incompatibility of this narrative device to his allegorical intention. For Spenser actually constructed his six books in three distinct ways, each of them at a more distant remove from the ideal of *in medias res* narration so facilely sketched in the letter and each of them moving finally to an *ab ovo* structure compatible with his allegory. Books I and II seem to answer best to his dictum that a poet is not an historiographer who "discourseth of affayres orderly as they were donne" but one who thrusteth into the middest, even where it most concerneth him, and there recoursing to the thinges forepaste, and divining of thinges to come, maketh a pleasing analysis of all.[6]

Both books begin in "the middest"; they both "recourse to thinges forepaste" by the agency of the delegated narrators: Una in Book I and Guyon in Book II. Yet even in these most orthodox of books, the *in medias res* strategy seems to be more mechanical than organic. One is not convinced that the perfunctory "recoursing to thinges forepaste" could not have been as successfully, indeed more successfully, accomplished by the omniscient voice at the beginning of each book, particularly since any recourse by way of the voice of a specific narrator necessarily subjects the allegory to the un-allegorical implications of restricted narration. It is almost impossible to forget that when Una tells her story in Book I, for example, she represents a character in a story speaking from a limited point of view. But once Spenser has constructed his book on an *in medias res* plan, he has no choice but recourse to things "forepaste" by the agency of such a restricted voice. It is at this point that the expectations of restricted narration clash with the demands of allegory.

Books III and IV are also *in medias res* structures, but with some significant differences. First of all, and this is an obvious difference, unlike Books I and II, which are each self-contained, autonomous narratives, III and IV represent a continuum and can be considered as one book instead of two.[7] It is true, as Leicester Bradner points out,[8] that much of the significant complication of Books III and IV is not resolved until Book V, but I would prefer seeing V as a new departure which accidentally inherits some of the narrative residue of III and IV. More important than this "long since cancelled" problem, however, is the one curious quality that sets III and IV apart from the more regular Books I and II. Although the poet begins III-IV *in medias res* with the forester's pursuit of Florimel (or one may prefer to consider the Florimel flight as a transitional incident contrived to set Britomart on her adventures free of Arthur's and Guyon's company and Britomart's experiences at Malecasta's castle as the real beginning of the book), Spenser does *not* return to the prerequisite action by way of a delegated narrator. The

---

[6]   Edmund Spenser, *The Complete Poetical Works of Spenser*, ed. R. E. Neil Dodge (Cambridge, Mass., 1936), p. 137.
[7]   The reasons are too well known to be repeated here. See Josephine Bennett, *The Evolution of The Faerie Queene* (New York, 1960 ed.), Chapters I and II.
[8]   Leicester Bradner, *Edmund Spenser and The Faerie Queene* (Chicago, 1948), Chapter IV.

long account of Britomart's "mirror" infatuation with Arthegal, her visit incognito to Merlin's cell, his subsequent advice to her and epic teleologizing – all expository material that in the hands of another epic writer would have been delegated to a restricted narrator – is here, curiously enough, related in the *omniscient* voice. Spenser reveals himself either as totally unmindful of the chronological absurdity of breaking into one's own narrative with an interruption that does violence to the normal time of the action (without dramatically justifying that temporal manipulation) or as having to choose between an allegory-shattering restricted narration and an allegory-preserving omniscient flashback.

Moreover, the interruption here in question is not that kind of occasional and brief temporal manipulation which any omniscient narrator will indulge in from time, but rather a substantial segment of Book III – a full 97 stanzas.[9] It is ten times longer than Una's narration and twenty times longer than Guyon's. It is equal in proportionate length and expository importance to the restricted narrations of Ulysses, Aeneas, Calasiris, Musidorus and Pyrocles, and Raphael in their respective epics. By all the norms of narrative propriety and logic, by all the conventions which Spenser inherited from epic poets and critics, this narration should have been placed in the restricted voice. Because it was not, it makes for a situation of extraordinary awkwardness in which an *in medias res* structure allows for no correlative restricted voice to narrate action prerequisite to its "artificial" beginning. For the above reasons, therefore, I would designate Books III and IV as the second distinct type of structure in *The Faerie Queene*, one that observes the demands of *in medias res* with even less concern than Books I and II.

The third example of structural type is one that would have saved Spenser considerable trouble if he had used it in all his books instead of attempting to invest his work with pseudo-epic dignity by a mechanical adherence to *in medias res*. That structure is the *ab ovo* narrative upon which Books V and VI are built. I interpret these books as the most successfully handled architectonically because their design seems most compatible with Spenser's narrative and allegorical intention and least dictated by a convention that he apparently understood only dimly. This is not to say, of course, that Spenser's commitment to an *ab ovo* structure necessarily insured unqualified success. Critics of Book V, for example, have rightfully pointed not only to the too transparent political allegory

---

9   III, ii, 17 to III, iv, 61. For an example of the occasional omniscient flashback, see *Paradise Lost*, IV, 925-945.

contained therein [10] but also to the rigid control which that political allegory wields over the direction of the plot.[11] Yet, in spite of the obviously unsuccessful incidents revolving around Gerioneo in Cantos X and XI, incidents that seem to get in the way of the climactic progression from Duessa's trial at Mercilla's court to Arthegal's beheading of Grantorto at Irena's land, the book possesses a structural simplicity that III and IV with their pseudo-manipulation of time cannot match. In Book V, "there is only one plot, that of the knight of justice. Except for Britomart's journey to Radigund and Arthur's defeat of Belge's foes, the book is confined to episodes of which Artegall is the integral presence. . . . Perhaps Spenser's theme has dictated the new mode of narrative. It does not seem proper that a book devoted to justice should play games with the reader's attention." [12]

Book VI too shares something of the relative structural simplicity of Book V. As in V, the poet does not interpolate the necessary exposition later in the narrative but proceeds immediately in the first few cantos to explain the identity and background of the knight and the nature of his quest. The differences in expository technique between V and VI are interesting, though not really significant. In V, the omniscient voice narrates the expository details – Arthegal's upbringing by Astrea, her choice of Talus as his companion, and the quest which Gloriana assigns to him – without the use of dialogue; in VI, Calidore's background and the nature of his quest are explained both by the omniscient voice and by Calidore himself in conversation with Arthegal. The really important consideration here, however, is that Spenser has abandoned, except for the occasional tangential stories, the device of postponing exposition to later cantos, and by this abandoning of an unworkable device has freed his allegory from the pressures and demands of restricted narration.

3

Unlike the *New Arcadia* where Sidney's experimentation with restricted voice led him into a variety of delegated narrations, Spenser's internal stories can be safely divided into only two groups: the primary or major delegated and the tangential. Even with this simplified distinction, however, the critic feels hesitant to employ the terms because in Spenser what should function logically as "major" narrations are often sub-

[10]   H. S. V. Jones, *A Spenser Handbook* (New York, 1947), p. 261.
[11]   Bradner, p. 92 ff.
[12]   Leo Kirschbaum, "Introduction", *Edmund Spenser, Selected Poetry* (New York, 1961), p. xxxi.

ordinated in their development to the tangential. We witness the curious imbalance in Book II, for example, of the Squire's tangential story being longer than Guyon's primary story by some 105 lines,[13] or the unusual situation in Book I of Fradubio's story having more impact on the main action than Una's.[14] Be that as it may, it is necessary to preserve the distinction in terms because, despite the frequent imbalances, the exigencies of *in medias res* structure determine that some restricted narrations necessarily play a major role and others a minor. Spenser's frequent inability to maintain the distinction will be evident in the book-by-book analysis of the restricted narration.

Book I

The structure of Book I has been the most universally praised of all the six books in *The Faerie Queene*. Josephine Bennett sees it as "a complete and satisfactory whole":

> It has a beginning in the separation of Redcrosse from Una; a middle, including a climax and a reversal, in the struggle with Orgoglio; and an end in the final victory of Redcrosse and his betrothal to Una. ... The book remains a complete structural unit which has been fitted into Spenser's large plans rather than evolved out of them.[15]

Other critics have praised its careful organization in "proceeding systematically through complication to its climax in Canto VIII, and then through resolution to its *denouement* at the close".[16]

But in relation to the *in medias res* tradition, at least, such praise must be qualified. Spenser did not choose to open his book with an immediate exposition of Red Cross's quest as he did with regard to both Arthegal and Calidore. Such an *ab ovo* opening admittedly has its disadvantages. The progress of the complication is slower; suspense is directed forward to the resolution but not backward to the restricted exposition; and those manipulations which make for chronological realism are made unnecessary. But the narrative advantages which are attendant upon an *in medias res* opening carry with them certain obligations later in the action: namely, a scrupulously "voiced" use of the restricted narrator. Spenser, unhappily, wished to gain the initial advantages without later wrestling with the obligations.

In the area of restricted narration, then, Book I contains one primary

---

[13]   Squire's story: II, iv, 17 ff.; Guyon's: II, ii, 40 ff.
[14]   Fradubio's story: I, ii, 34 ff.; Una's: I, vii, 42 ff.
[15]   Bennett, p. 108.
[16]   Jones, p. 150.

delegated story – Una's to Arthur in Canto VII; one tangential narration – Fradubio's to Red Cross in Canto II; and three more stories that defy exact classification. One of these is Arthur's account of his meeting with the Faerie Queen in Canto IX, a story that might have been handled just as easily in the omniscient voice. Another is Sir Trevisan's account in the same canto of his meeting with Sir Terwin and Despair; the third is Contemplation's "once and future" story in Canto X of Red Cross as St. George. The latter two could be dismissed immediately as not genuine delegated narrations, for they really represent one side of a dialogue rather than self-contained, uninterrupted autonomous narrations with a beginning, middle and end. Yet, as hybrid as they seem, they both possess the functional character of clearly delegated narrations, particularly as they relate to the effect of the recitation on the main action. In both instances, Trevisan's story and Contemplation's wield an effect on the direction of the main action and on the development of Red Cross's character that the theoretically more important stories do not. For Trevisan predisposes Red Cross to despair and near suicide, and Contemplation, by his prophecies about St. George, disposes Red Cross to spiritual preparedness for his battles with the dragon. Fradubio's story, a genuine tangential narration, does the same thing. Its function is to anticipate Red Cross's fall by the instrumentality of Duessa. Ironically, the witch of whom Fradubio speaks and for whom he had left Fraelissa is at that moment the very person riding by Red Cross's side and for whose affection he had left Una.

Compared to the extraordinarily functional nature of these mere tangential stories, the one story that should work as the major delegated narration of Book I – Una's – is curiously reticent and relatively unsuccessful. On the allegorical level, of course, its function is clear: Una's parents, the King and Queen of Eden (Adam and Eve), are put in bondage (original sin) by the strength of Satan and it is Una (the Christian faith) who is to be instrumental in freeing them. But on the narrative level, the demands of allegory, as we have already seen, tend to militate against her restricted knowledge; she lends no significant details to the exposition about Gloriana's court (which is probably the most serious failing [17]); she indulges in no restricted characterization

---

[17] The most charitable qualification one can make in this judgment is that the rich exposition necessary to each hero might have been supplied in Book XII if the poem had been completed. Spenser seems to indicate this intention in his letter to Raleigh: "The beginning ... of my history, if it were to be told by an historiographer, should be the twelfth booke ... where I devise that the Faerie Queene kept her annuall feast xii. dayes, upon which xii. severall dayes, the oc-

(which is a cardinal function of all major restricted narrators in other epics); and her story does next to nothing to further the main action. Although the dramatic modulation from the omniscient voice to hers is convincing enough (Arthur tenderly trying to learn from her the cause of her sorrow), once the modulation has been accomplished, the subsequent effect does not seem worth the effort. Her account mechanically rehearses the facts of the dragon's siege, her seeking out of Gloriana's court for redress and the Queen's assigning of Red Cross as her succor. All these facts have allegorical significance, but as narrative episodes, which a Homer or Milton would have exploited to the fullest in three or four books, Spenser assigns to Una in a mere 86 lines. Those nuances of voice that we saw achieved in the restricted narrators of other epics are never developed. Whatever function the recitation as a whole might have served either in furthering the main action, or revealing character, or presenting an episodic microcosm to the macrocosm of the main action is necessarily shut off. Una tells her story and then it is over. The narrative reverberations that extended to the distant books of Homer's epic as a result of Ulysses' narration Spenser is deprived from sounding in this similar situation because of the allegorical muffle.

Book II

A. C. Hamilton, in the company of other critics, is quite correct in seeing Book II as parallel in structure to Book I.

In each the knight who represents a particular virtue (Holiness, Temperance) leaves the court of the Faerie Queen with a guide (Una, the Palmer) and later defeats two chief antagonists (Sansfoy and Sansjoy, Pyrochles and Cymochles); upon being separated from his guide, he enters a place of temptation (the house of Pride, the cave of Mammon) and later falls. Then being rescued by Arthur and united with his guide, he enters a place of instruction (the house of Holiness, the castle of Alma) and finally fulfills his adventure (killing the Dragon, destroying the Bower of Bliss).[18]

---

casions of the xii. severall adventures hapned, which being undertaken by xii. severall knights, are in these xii. books severally handled and discoursed."

But even such a grand reprise of exposition in the final book would not have supplied the need for immediate revelation of the hero's background within his book itself. The delay would have been intolerable, the need for exposition by this time no longer pressing. Indeed, Mrs. Bennett suggests that the reason Spenser omitted the letter to Raleigh in the 1596 edition of the poem may have been due to a desire to suppress some features of his plan, especially the expository designs of the twelfth book. See p. 37.

[18] A. C. Hamilton, *The Structure of Allegory in The Faerie Queene* (Oxford, 1961), p. 90.

But if Spenser parallels structural virtues, he also parallels structural defects. Having allowed Guyon to "thrust into the middest" by coming across Amavia near death (Archimago's attempt to trick Guyon into battle with Red Cross is really a transition from the first book), Spenser must ultimately allow his hero to return to the real beginning of his story. And as Douglas Bush has observed, the result is an unhappy one.

In the second canto Medina entertains Guyon – the "mean" has no heart to be captured by a guest! – and her desire to hear the story of his adventures corresponds to that of Dido. In the *Aeneid,* of course, we have the structural device of recapitulation that follows the plunge *in medias res*; but Guyon has no epic narrative to recount, and Spenser seems merely to have taken over a bit of technique for which he has no real use.[19]

Guyon has no epic narrative to recount because he is the allegorical representation of temperance as well as a character in his own right. Any of the obliquenesses and ambivalences of restricted narration that we heard from the other epic heroes would have been totally inappropriate on the didactic lips of Temperance, whose teachings must necessarily be clear and unequivocal. On the literal level, part of the difficulty may have been caused by Spenser's indecision as to what really happened at the Faerie Court. In his letter to Raleigh, he indicated that the Palmer arrived at Gloriana's court, bearing a baby with bloody hands and asking for a knight to avenge the deaths of the child's parents slain by Acrasia. Guyon's narration, however, indicates only that the Palmer wished redress for "grievous mischiefes which a wicked Fay/ Had wrought". The detail of the orphaned child in the actual execution of Book II is narrated *after* and not before the *in medias res* beginning. At any rate, what should have operated as a major delegated story by the chief character about himself fizzles, even more flatly than Una's story in Book I, to a few perfunctory stanzas about expository details.

As in Book I, also, the tangential narrations seem more fully wrought than the major.[20] Amavia's story in Canto I of Acrasia's wickedness in enchanting Mordant is vivid enough (particularly since it is from the point of view of the abused wife), but the spectacle of a dying woman indulging in rhetorical "dawn" poetry indicates that Spenser never excercised a great deal of control over his restricted voice. The other tangential narration in Book II is as close to Sidney's use of this story as

[19] Douglas Bush, *Mythology and the Renaissance Tradition in English Poetry* (New York, 1932), pp. 102-103.
[20] I continue to use the distinction in terms between major delegated narration and tangential narration reviewed in Chapter III, although by now it should be obvious that in *The Faerie Queene* the distinction is more nominal than real.

any in *The Faerie Queene*. Unlike the tangential narrations already seen, in which all of the characters are at least indirectly involved with the progress of the main action, the squire Phedon's story concerns people whose fates are totally independent of the main action: his beloved Claribell, the disguised Pyrene, and the false friend Philemon. One is immediately reminded of Sidney's tangential narration of Argalus and Parthenia whose fates also are independent of the main action. The major difference between them, however, is that whereas Sidney finally returns his lovers to the main action in Book III, Spenser does not allow his tangents to cross even the periphery of his central plot.

Books III-IV

As indicated earlier, Books III-IV contain that most unorthodox of Spenserian architectonic devices – the omniscient flashback. Because they include a number of important characters revolving around Britomart and because most of the exposition about these characters is handled in the same way, Books III-IV contain almost as many omniscient flashbacks as there are sets of central characters. Britomart, as I have demonstrated already, is assigned a flashback of 97 stanzas early in Canto III; but other characters get a substantial portion as well, much more indeed than in the orthodox restricted flashbacks of Books I and II. Amoret and Belphoebe, Britomart's chaste "foils", are allowed 49 stanzas of omniscient exposition in Canto VI (the Garden of Adonis is included here). Cambell and Triamond, the putative centers of Book IV, receive a full 72 stanzas in Cantos II and III.

But the unusual length and frequency of the omniscient flashbacks do not help to explain their essential awkwardness. One still feels, as the omniscient narrator halts the forward direction of the story in order to fill in the background details, that he had simply forgotten to tell us about Britomart and her group when they were first introduced, that the flashback, in short, was an afterthought. And his interruption is no simple pluperfect backstep which all epic writers and even omniscient novelists occasionally take. Rather, these flashbacks are complete stories in their own right (as are all restricted episodes) with beginnings, middles and ends. When the expected voicing of this kind of story, then, is not delegated to a restricted narrator, the reader's reaction is a puzzled one. Why manipulate time when such a manipulation cannot be logically or dramatically motivated, and when the one really significant effect of such a manipulation – the presence of a restricted narrator – is not exploited?

These temporal improprieties represent only one aspect of the narrative awkwardnesses resulting from the omniscient flashback. Another is the problem of dramatic justification for the telling of the episodes in the first place. When one recalls how carefully most restricted narrations are prepared for in other epics, Spenser's modulations into his omniscient flashbacks are almost ludicrously curt and abrupt. For example, although Belphoebe had already played a substantial role in the events of Book III (she had even been introduced briefly in the Bragadocchio "love" scene in Book II), Spenser waits until the middle of Book III to interpolate exposition about her and Amoret; and when he does, it is with the absurd tone of "listen-children-and-you-shall-hear":

> It were a goodly storie, to declare,
> By what straunge accident faire Chrysogone
> Conceiv'd these infants . . .
>   (III, vi, 5)

And at one point in the Cambell-Triamond exposition, Spenser, feeling the need for some dramatic transition from present to past tense, even tries epic invocation to Chaucer, his "muse":

> . . . but through infusion sweete
> Of thine owne spirit, which doth in me survive,
> I follow here the footing of thy feete,
> That with thy meanings so I may thee rather meete.
>   (IV, ii, 34)

The necessary absence of an auditor in each of these omniscient flashbacks results in a further structural awkwardness. As we have observed before, the internal stories of all major delegated narrators tend to forward the main plot, because the recitation of the episode itself moves the internal auditor to some kind of significant action. Pamela and Philoclea fall in love with the princes because Musidorus and Pyrocles recite their own story. Adam, by virtue of Raphael's narration, is moved, ironically, to the very sins against which the angel had admonished him. But when the large expository narration is directed not to an internal character but to the reader himself, the flashback can serve no such catalystic effect on the subsequent main action. Spenser merely picks up the thread where he had momentarily dropped it, at the point where he had attempted to weave the omniscient exposition into his general fabric. But the thread stitches loosely; and woof and warp, for this patch of narration at least, unbraid.

Before I comment on the tangential narrations of Books III and IV, I should direct a brief word to the only restricted narration in these books that might be judged as major: Scudamour's story of his winning of Amoret at the Temple of Venus. The difficulty in ascribing the adjective "major" to this narrative results from Spenser's decision in the 1596 edition of *The Faerie Queene* to continue the adventures of Amoret and Scudamour into Book IV and not to terminate the story with the reunion of the lovers. The intermittent appearance of these two characters in search of each other results in a kind of competition with the titular heroes – Triamond and Cambell – and with the rest of the large cast that diminishes the stature of the lovers as major figures in Book IV. When, therefore, at the end of the book Scudamour launches into a long delegated narration about his winning of Amoret, the reader feels that what he is saying is both tardy and ineffectual. Why Spenser chose to relate this particular story in the restricted voice when he related all the others of III-IV by way of the omniscient flashback is not clear, particularly when we remember Mrs. Bennett's suggestion that this episode is a formal allegory that could have been attached to any heroine.[21] Equally inexplicable is the reason for his placing this piece of exposition the distance of an entire book away from the one major incident concerning the principals – the Busirane imprisonment of Amoret and her subsequent freeing by Britomart. Distant from its "parent" action as it is, it fails not only as exposition but also as episode affecting the forward direction of the main action. Curiously, Amoret is among the group of people to whom Scudamour is narrating the story. Yet no reunion of the two lovers is effected by it; nor indeed do they even recognize each other. And in the next canto the omniscient voice, oblivious to the potential significance of the Scudamour narration, shifts its emphasis to Florimel in Proteus's dungeon.

Unlike the omniscient flashbacks and the one misplaced restricted narration, the tangential stories of III-IV show a more even hand in control. Although the Squire of Dames' story of the sexual monsters, Argante and Olliphant (III, vii, 47-60), seems remote from the narrator's own subsequent involvement in the main action, other tangential stories blend smoothly into the Ariostan counterpoint of III-IV. The Paridell narration, for example, about his Trojan genealogy (III, ix, 41-51) seems particularly appropriate as an introduction to the subsequent action: Paridell (Paris) abducting Malbecco's (Menelaus's) wife, Hellenore (Helen). And the one story that some critics have read as a better illustration of the titular virtue of Book IV than the story of

---

[21] P. 169.

Cambel and Triamond – the Placidas-Amyas episode (IV, viii, 47-62) – is probably the most successfully handled restricted narration in III-IV. Narrated by Placidas to Arthur (who has just rescued Amoret and Aemylia from Lust and Placidas himself from Corflambo), it complements Aemylia's brief account of her romance with Amyas (the Squire of Low Degree) by seeing it from the male's point of view, yet still recognizing the essentially carnal nature of young, precipitous love unrestrained by parental guidance or social propriety. Moreover, its very recitation has a powerful effect on the main action by stirring Arthur to free the imprisoned Amyas from Poena's dungeon and restore him, now chastened by suffering, to Aemylia.

Books V and VI

W. J. B. Owen's passing comment on Books V and VI implicitly identifies their structure in terms to which this study is addressed. "They were modelled, more or less, on I and II", he writes, "but on I and II as stories of knightly quests, *not as miniature epic structures* [22] (italics mine). There is no question that Spenser's plot is considerably simplified in Books V and VI. Incident follows upon incident without the confusing contrapuntal qualities of III and IV and without the pseudo-epic expositions of I and II. For the first time in *The Faerie Queene*, Spenser abjures the *in medias res* and makes no artificial distinction between real beginning and narrated beginning. We learn of the backgrounds and the quests of Arthegal and Calidore in the very first stanzas of the very first cantos.

Such an abandoning of the *in medias res* produces structural consequences peculiar to an *ab ovo* narrative. The most important result is that since the bulk of the exposition is covered immediately by the omniscient voice there is no need for flashback, and hence, except for the tangential narrations, no need for the restricted voice at all. The artistic advantages that had been gained by the presence of the restricted voice are, of course, lost. But Spenser had seldom exploited these advantages: through his peculiar brand of *in medias res* structure, he had juggled time without really manipulating it functionally, and had allowed for restricted voices that seldom sounded truly restricted. For *The Faerie Queene*, therefore, the abandonment of *in medias res,* because its use had been so ineffectual in earlier books, results in architectonic improvement with a hylomorphic unity of narrative base and allegorical

[22] "The Structure of *The Faerie Queene*", *PMLA*, LXVIII (Dec., 1953), 1098, n. 46.

superstructure.[23] True, a less sophisticated structure follows upon a more complex structure, but then unpretentious simplicity is always preferable to pseudo-complexity.

The only extended use of restricted voice in Books V and VI is to be found in the tangential narrations, but unlike the similar narrations of the previous books, they make no important use of it. Because these books are *ab ovo* in structure, with a minimum of movement away from the central character and an episodic type of plot which moves the hero almost uninterruptedly from one adventure to another, the occasion for full-blown tangential narrations as we saw in Sidney is limited. Indeed, all of the stories in Book V that are related by various subordinate characters about their own difficulties turn into complication in the main action, complication which the hero takes upon himself to resolve. There are five such narrations in Book V.[24] Each of the complications related therein crosses Arthegal's path and each is resolved by his instrumentality. Unlike Sidney's tangential narrations, these stories are totally dependent on the protagonist of the main action; and because they are less tangential than Sidney's there is little, if any, real autonomy of restricted voice. The reader feels that a brief omniscient flashback in the pluperfect would have served to complicate the main action equally well.

Because Book VI is *ab ovo*, the use of tangential narration is somewhat similar to that of V. The squire's story of Briana's shearing off the locks of passing ladies and knights, a bit of exposition that is narrated tangentially, becomes complication in the main plot. When Calidore moves against this form of discourtesy by slaying Maleffort and conciliating Briana and Crudor, the complication is resolved. Unlike Book V, however, some stories become more tangential than those serving merely as complication for the main action, because Spenser in this book allowed a certain amount of contrapuntal design. It is not the same quality of highly "polyphonic" counterpoint as in Book IV where many tales moved in constant fugue; but from the middle of Canto III to the

---

[23] One may complain with Mrs. Bennett that the incidents of Book V are formal and disconnected and that the result is a "peculiarly wooden and inflexible structure" (p. 178), but it would seem that for allegorical purposes a highly contrapuntal plot militates against the allegory which should be to some extent clear and sharp.

[24] The squire's account of Sanglier's abduction of his lady; Bracidas's account of his eroded island; Terpine's story about Radigund's amazonian fury against the Knights of Maidenhead; Samient's story about Mercilla and her implacable enemies; Burbon's story of Flourdelis' inconstancy.

end of Canto VIII Calidore is removed from the scene and the omniscient focus fades to Calepine and Serena. Since their adventures are
themselves a type of tangent from the main plot, any further restricted
narration that their stories occasion (Matilde's account of her childless
marriage to Sir Bruin, for example) leads still farther away from the
main action. As in the rest of *The Faerie Queene*, however, tangential
narration here serves only as a complicating device in the main action
and never as an occasion to experiment with the nuances of restricted
voice.

4

The reasons for Spenser's failure to appropriate to *The Faerie Queene*
the narrative strategies resulting from an *in medias res* structure (with
the consequent failure to utilize the subtleties of restricted voice) can be
explained in a postscript by reference to Mrs. Bennett's well-known
theory of the poem's composition. We have already investigated the
debilitating contradiction between allegory and *in medias res*, of course,
but Mrs. Bennett's theory will add a slightly new dimension to the
explanation.

She contends, despite some scholarly arguments against the kind of
study that would pretend to trace accurately this work's evolution,[25]
that no theory of seriatim composition is tenable in relation to *The
Faerie Queene*. Because much of Spenser's early Ariostan imitation is
to be found in Books III and IV, rather than in I and II, she insists
that it is reasonable to "look in the more Ariosto-like books for evidence
of Spenser's Ariosto-like beginnings".[26] Books I and II, representing a
more classical type of narrative technique: namely, Virgil's, were produced later, probably not until very late in the 1580-90 period.[27] The
reason for his moving away from Ariostan contrapuntalism to the more
Virgilian structure of Books I and II was probably Gabriel Harvey's
disapproval of the conjectural first version of *The Faerie Queene*, which
presumably began as an adaptation of Chaucer's *Sir Thopas* and was

[25] W. J. B. Owen denies the possibility of pinpointing revision by internal examination: ". . . a consideration of the poem as we have it shows that the notion
of 'revision' on a large scale, leading to narrative discrepancies and to general
disorder and formlessness, may well be one to which no meaning can be attached;
for the presence of narrative discrepancies, the critic's main instrument for the
detection of revision, can be explained otherwise than as a result of revision."
P. 1086.
[26] P. 45.
[27] P. 115.

continued in the lighter vein of Ariosto.[28] Spenser's ultimate intention, then, was probably to transform his romance-like Ariostan imitations into a work worthy of the name *epic*.

To become the English Virgil, Spenser had to invest his work with epic dignity by utilizing certain devices of epic construction. Among the conventions that he must have recognized, both in actual classical examples like the *Odyssey* and the *Aeneid* and in critical pronouncements like Minturno's and Scaliger's, was the *in medias res* beginning. Spenser no doubt began effecting an *in medias res* transformation in his work when early reactions to the poem (like Harvey's) were less than enthusiastic. If Mrs. Bennett is correct in theorizing that portions of Books III and IV represent Spenser's earliest attempts at composing his work, it would follow that in attempting to transpose an Ariostan contrapuntal narrative into a "Virgilized" Ariostan, *in medias res* narrative, Spenser probably fell into crudities in his first attempt that he refined away in later starts. Among these crudities, as I have already indicated, were the use of the omniscient flashback and the major delegated narration of Scudamour that functioned at an impossible distance from its correlative major incident in the main action.

No such blunders were allowed in Books I and II. Like a good, classical epic writer, Spenser began *in medias res* and this time allowed a *nuntius* to "recount things done in former time or other place". The difficulty even with this act of conformity to the convention was that Spenser did not understand the device well enough and failed to exploit the host of narrative advantages related to it (largely because of the allegorical intention which neutralized its potential effectiveness). The artistic results of this imposition of a pre-determined form on a substance not hylomorphically related to it have already been reviewed: "Spenser seems merely to have taken over a technique for which he had no real use." [29]

It would be an interesting, though entirely unprovable, theory, that Books V and VI represent Spenser's mature realization, after experimenting with *in medias res* design for some 25,000 lines, that his narrative strength did not lie in that area; that whatever perfunctory obedience he had earlier afforded to that epic convention resulted in a narrative awkwardly related to his allegory. In Books V and VI, he makes no pretense to *in medias res,* restrains some of the more exuberant examples of Ariostan contrapuntal design that characterized the struc-

---

[28]   P. 38.
[29]   Bush, p. 103.

tures of Books III and IV, and proceeds entirely in *ab ovo* fashion, content to let his characters speak briefly only in the tangential narrations and in the normal dialogue. The results, though not as sophisticated and challenging from the aspects of restricted voice, manipulated time and general structural complexity, nevertheless contain a simple integrity that preserves the union of narrative and allegory.

EPILOGUE

This study has attempted to enunciate and demonstrate a number of theories about narrative techniques in the epic poem by addressing an ancient narrative tradition in modern critical terms. Central to the meaning of the whole dissertation is the judgment that a relationship exists between a writer's commitment to an *in medias res* structure and his ultimate use of restricted voice. If the Renaissance and eighteenth-century critics of the epic established rigid conventions which prescribed the use of the *in medias res* and the *nuntius*, it was because, with or without their awareness of the fact, one does not exist without the other. The omniscient voice, thrusting into the middle of an action, usually proceeds to relate incidents of the main action in a seriatim manner. But having rushed "into the middest", the omniscient voice is forced to return to that action which it has deliberately overlooked by having begun at an "artificial" beginning. Because the omniscient voice, by its very nature, is all-knowing, super-logical and detached from the material it is narrating, any return to incidents temporally and causally prerequisite to the main action must be logically and dramatically motivated. Whereas a restricted narrator may violate time with impunity because his assimilation and transmission of experience is determined and limited by finite, fallible mental processes, an omniscient narrator may not. Whereas a restricted narrator may very well forget, interrupt himself and return to a previous incident without doing violence to the integrity of his knowing process, an omniscient narrator cannot forget. Because his is not an experiential knowledge but one freed from time, his communication must of necessity be logical, causal, serial; and his "return" to the prerequisite action must of necessity be motivated by some incident in the normal action which is directed backwards to a previous time. It is at this point that the omniscient narrator gives away, or delegates, his voice to a character in the story who can return to the prerequisite action. It is at this point that restricted narration begins in the epic poem; indeed, it probably was at this point that restricted narration began in Western Literature.

The narrative strategies that become possible when this delegation takes place are too numerous to be repeated in a conclusion. An analysis of their function in the works discussed constitute, of course, the bulk of this study. But for the sake of recapitulation, some might be reviewed. First, the delegation from omniscient to restricted voice must be smoothly modulated. This transition involves both a believable reason for an internal character to relate his story and also a believable reason for an audience to want to hear it. Second, because the omniscient voice has logically suspended its activity while a lesser speaker has taken over, the story which the new voice narrates must be directed both backward and forward. That is to say, the restricted story should function both as exposition and, by the very fact of its recitation, as an incident in its own right. Thus, the artificial distinction that the eighteenth-century critics were fond of making between incident (or fable) and episode is only logically and not ontologically valid. Episode can be considered as episode when the restricted narrator rehearses details of prerequisite action; but episode is merely one more incident in the main action when the effects of its recitation *by* a character in the main plot *to* an audience in the main plot are counted.

Maintaining the integrity of the restricted voice, once the omniscient voice has delegated its function, is a further consideration of major importance. If the new voice merely repeats the omniscience of the old, but in a different *persona*, then no real delegation has taken place. There must be, during the tenure of this delegation from omniscience to restriction, an "epistemological" adherence to the new narrator's limited extent of knowledge. And this limitation must be preserved scrupulously, or the new narration becomes a mere *alter vox* for the omniscient voice.

Such a maintenance of restricted integrity makes possible, among other things, a means of oblique characterization not open to the omniscient voice, the possibility of creating suspense both retroactive and forward, the introduction of subtle, functional irony, the development of a stylistic quality distinct from that proper to the omniscient voice, and a microcosmic paralleling or foreshadowing of episode to the macrocosm of the main action. Indeed, the narrative advantages open to the modern novelist who writes from a restricted point of view were in some way offered to the epic poet as soon as he committed himself to the *in medias res* structure.

It is a curiosity of literary history that the epic poet who took fullest advantage of these opportunities was Homer, who made them possible. The *Odyssey* was the first epic poem that began *in medias res*. And despite its oral formulaic character and extraordinary length, its execution in this regard is superior to that of any of those poems which looked back to its structure as a prototype. Certainly, Virgil in the *Aeneid*, for all his brilliance in other areas of narrative, makes only a perfunctory gesture at utilizing the techniques. Indeed, it might almost be claimed that those post-Classical epic writers who looked back to Homer and Virgil and emulated the latter instead of the former were only partially introduced to the narrative strategies resulting from *in medias res*. For if Virgil's use of the Dido episode, quasi-adventitious as it is to the main action, was recognized as the classical epic "model", then the poet emulating Virgil would have been unaware of the more sophisticated possibilities of *in medias res* structure contained in the *Odyssey*.

This theory, of course, is unworkable, because it would be impossible to do a source study on our English epic writers in order to determine whether the Homeric or Virgilian influence worked more fully on them. Furthermore, there is no assurance that mere exposure to a superior model would necessarily effect a superior performance. The visitations of genius, fortunately, are more democratic than that. Nevertheless, it is interesting to note that the English epic writer most influenced by Virgil, Spenser, was the least successful in exploiting the *in medias res* possibilities, and he who know Homer better than any of his race, Milton, was the most successful practitioner of this technique.[1]

If the critical investigations in this study are valid, it is clear that of the three major examples of epic production in English literature, only Spenser failed to enrich his work by imposing an *in medias res* structure on it. Sidney, despite his frequent erratic handling of the convention, particularly as it applied to the problem of complication, demonstrated at the same time a remarkable skill in transforming the romance-like *Old Arcadia* into the epic-like *New Arcadia* by means of the *in medias res* revision. Unlike Spenser, whose motive for effecting a similar revision in his work was ostensibly prompted by a desire to conform to the tradition rather than by any artistic recognition of its value, Sidney shows a particularly sensitive awareness of the subtle narrative techniques deriving from *in medias res*. In the areas of oblique characterization and functional use of episodes in particular, Sidney's artistry has been largely overlooked.

[1] James H. Hanford, *A Milton Handbook* (New York, 1946), see p. 177 and pp. 248-249.

Milton, probably because he worked with the genre of literary epic rather than with heroic romance, was clearly the most successful English epic poet using the *in medias res* technique. Whereas Sidney diluted some of his *in medias res* effectiveness by directing it into the involuted complications of the heroic romance and Spenser tried unsuccessfully to join an already brilliant allegory to it, Milton restored the "complex" simplicity of the device by returning to a purer type of epic poem. In the area of functional use of episodes, oblique characterization, motivated delegation of voices, stylistic distinction between voices, and parallel relationships between episodes and incidents, Milton is unsurpassed in the English epic and only surpassed in world literature by Homer himself.

WORKS CITED

Aquinas, St. Thomas, *Summa Theologica* (= *Great Books of the Western World*, vol. 19) (Chicago, 1952).

Aristotle, *Introduction to Aristotle*, ed. Richard McKeon (New York, 1947).

Bassett, Samuel Eliot, *The Poetry of Homer* (Berkeley, Calif., 1938).

Bennett, Josephine Waters, *The Evolution of "The Faerie Queene"* (New York, 1960).

Berger, Harry, Jr., *The Allegorical Temper* (New Haven, 1957).

Bloom, Edward A., "The Allegorical Principle", *Journal of English Literary History*, XVIII (1951), 163-190.

Boas, Frederick S., *Sir Philip Sidney* (London, 1955).

Booth, Wayne, *The Rhetoric of Fiction* (Chicago, 1961).

Bowra, C. M., *From Virgil to Milton* (London, 1957).

Bowra, C. M., *Heroic Poetry* (London, 1952).

Bowra, C. M., *Tradition and Design in the "Iliad"* (Oxford, 1930).

Bradner, Leicester, *Edmund Spenser and "The Faerie Queene"* (Chicago, 1948).

Bray, René, *La Formation de la Doctrine Classique en France* (Paris, 1931).

Broadbent, J. B., "Milton's Rhetoric", *Modern Philology*, LVI (1959), 224-242.

Bush, Douglas, *Mythology and the Renaissance Tradition in English Poetry* (New York, 1957).

Bush, Douglas, "Recent Criticism of *Paradise Lost*", *Philological Quarterly*, XXVIII (1949), 31-43.

Coleridge, Samuel Taylor, *Unpublished Letters of Samuel Taylor Coleridge*, ed. E. L. Griggs (New Haven, n.d.).

Daiches, David, *A Critical History of English Literature*, 2 vol. (New York, 1960).

Danby, John, *Poets on Fortune's Hill* (London, 1957).

Davis, Walter R. and Lanham, Richard A., *Sidney's "Arcadia"* (New Haven, 1965).

Dobell, Bertram, "New Light upon Sir Philip Sidney's *Arcadia*", *Quarterly Review*, CCXI (1909), 74-100.

Ferry, Anne Davidson, *Milton's Epic Voice* (Cambridge, Mass., 1963).

Friedman, Norman, "Point of View in Fiction: The Development of a Critical Concept", *PMLA*, LXX (1955), 1160-1184.

Frye, Northrop, *Anatomy of Criticism* (Princeton, 1957).

Gilbert, Alan H., *On the Composition of "Paradise Lost"* (Chapel Hill, 1947).

Gilbert, Alan H., "The Theological Basis of Satan's Rebellion and the function of Abdiel in *Paradise Lost*", *Modern Philology*, XL (1942), 19-42.

Greenlaw, Edwin A., "Sidney's *Arcadia* as an Example of Elizabethan Allegory", in *Kittredge Anniversary Papers* (1913), 327-337.

Griffin, Nathaniel, "Definition of Romance", *PMLA*, LXXVI (1922), 50-61.

Goldman, Marcus S., *Sir Philip Sidney and the "Arcadia"* (Urbana, Ill., 1934).

Guth, Hans P., "Allegorical Implications of Artifice in Spenser's *Faerie Queene*", *PMLA*, LXXVI (1961), 474-479.

Hagin, Peter, *The Epic Hero and the Decline of Epic Poetry* (Bern, 1964).

Hamilton, A. C., *Allegory in "The Faerie Queene"* (Oxford, 1961).

Hamilton, A. C., " 'Like Race to Runne': The Parallel Structure of *The Faerie Queene*, Books I and II", *PMLA*, LXXIII (1958), 327-334.

Hanford, James Holly, *A Milton Handbook* (New York, 1946).

Heliodorus, *An Ethiopian Romance*, transl. Moses Hadas (Ann Arbor, 1957).

Homer, *The "Iliad" of Homer and the "Odyssey"*, transl. Samuel Butler (= *Great Books of the Western World*, vol. 4) (Chicago, 1948).

Horace, *Horace: Satires, Epistles, Ars Poetica*, transl. H. Rushton Fairclough (London, 1926).

Hough, Graham, *A Preface to "The Faerie Queene"* (London, 1962).

James, Henry, *The Art of the Novel: Critical Prefaces*, ed. R. P. Blackmur (New York, 1934).

Johnson, Samuel, *Selected Prose and Poetry*, ed. Bertrand Bronson (New York, 1952).

Jones, H. S. V., *A Spenser Handbook* (New York, 1947).

Ker, W. P., *Epic and Romance* (New York, 1957).

Kermode, Frank, "Adam Unparadised", in *The Living Milton,* ed. Frank Kermode (London, 1960).

Lewis, C. S., *A Preface to "Paradise Lost"* (Oxford, 1942).

Lewis, C. S., *Sixteenth Century Literature* (Oxford, 1955).

Lewis, C. S., *The Allegory of Love* (New York, 1958).

MacAffrey, Isabel G., *"Paradise Lost" as "Myth"* (Cambridge, Mass., 1959).

Milton, John, *John Milton, Complete Poems and Major Prose*, ed. Merritt Y. Hughes (New York, 1957).

Myrick, Kenneth O., *Sir Philip Sidney as a Literary Craftsman* (Cambridge, Mass., 1935).

Nelson, William, *The Poetry of Edmund Spenser* (New York, 1963).

Owen, W. J. B., "The Structure of *The Faerie Queene*", *PMLA*, LXVIII (1953), 1079-1100.

Parker, M. Pauline, *The Allegory of "The Faerie Queene"* (Oxford, 1960).

Patterson, W. F., *Three Centuries of French Poetic Theory: A Critical History of the Chief Arts of Poetry in France (1328-1630)* (Ann Arbor, 1935).

Peter, John, *A Critique of "Paradise Lost"* (New York, 1960).

Plato, *The Dialogues of Plato*, transl. Benjamin Jowett (*Great Books of the Western World*, vol. 7) (Chicago, 1952).

Praz, Mario, "Sidney's Original *Arcadia*", *London Mercury*, XV (1927), 507-514.

Rees, Joan, "Fulke Greville and the Revisions of *Arcadia*", *Review of English Studies*, XVII (1966), 54-57.

Roche, Thomas P., Jr., *The Kindly Flame: A Study of the Third and Fourth Books of Spenser's "Faerie Queene"* (Princeton, 1964).

Ronsard, P. de, *Œuvres Complètes de P. de Ronsard*, ed. Prosper Blanchemain (Paris, 1858).

Rose, Mark, "Sidney's Womanish Man", *Review of English Studies*, XV (1964), 353-363.

Shawcross, John T., "The Balanced Structure of *Paradise Lost*", *Studies in Philology*, LXII (1965), 696-718.

Sidney, Sir Philip, *The Countesse of Pembrokes Arcadia*, ed. Albert Feuillerat, vol. 1 and 4 (Cambridge, 1927).

Southey, Robert, *The Poetical Works of Robert Southey* ("collected by himself"), vol. 1 (New York, n.d.).

Spenser, Edmund, *Selected Poetry*, ed. Leo Kirschbaum (New York, 1961).

Spenser, Edmund, *The Complete Poetical Works of Spenser*, ed. R. E. Dodge (Cambridge, Mass., 1936).

Svendsen, Kester, "Epic Address and Reference in *Paradise Lost*", *Philological Quarterly*, XXVIII (1949), 185-206.

Swedenberg, H. T., Jr., *The Theory of the Epic in England, 1650-1800* (= *University of California Publications in English*, vol. 15) (Berkeley, Calif., 1944).

Tillyard, E. M. W., *Studies in Milton* (London, 1951).

Tillyard, E. M. W., *The English Epic and its Background* (Oxford, 1954).

Toliver, Harold E., "Complicity of Voice in *Paradise Lost*", *Modern Language Quarterly*, XXV (1964), 153-170.

Tung, Mason, "The Abdiel Episode", *Studies in Philology*, LXII (1965), 595-609.

Virgil, *The Aeneid*, transl. C. D. Lewis (New York, 1952).

Waldock, A. J. A., *Paradise Lost and its Critics* (Gloucester, Mass., 1947).

Walzl, Florence L., "Milton's *Paradise Lost*, III, 150-166", *Explicator*, XX (1961), item 11.

Watson, J. R., "Divine Providence and the Structure of *Paradise Lost*", *Essays in Criticism*, XIV (1964), 148-155.

West, Robert H., *Milton and the Angels* (Athens, Ga., 1955).

Whaler, James, "Similes in Paradise Lost", *Modern Philology*, XXVIII (1931), 313-327.

Whitman, Cedric H., *Homer and the Heroic Tradition* (Cambridge, Mass., 1958).

Wilkie, Brian, *Romantic Poets and Epic Tradition* (Madison, Wis., 1965).

Wolff, S. L., *The Greek Romances in Elizabethan Prose Fiction* (New York, 1912).

Zandvoort, R. W., *Sidney's "Arcadia": A Comparison Between the Two Versions* (Amsterdam, 1929).

INDEX